With over 2 million copies of her books sold worldwide, number one *Sunday Times* bestseller Clare Mackintosh is the multi-award-winning author of *I Let You Go, I See You* and *Let Me Lie*. Clare's novels have been translated into over thirty-five languages and *I Let You Go* and *I See You* were selected for the Richard and Judy Book club.

Clare is patron of the Silver Star Society, a charity based at the John Radcliffe Hospital in Oxford, which supports parents experiencing high-risk or difficult pregnancies. She lives in North Wales with her husband and their three children.

For more information visit Clare's website www.claremackintosh.com or find her at www.facebook.com/ClareMackWrites or on Twitter @ClareMackint0sh.

A Cotswold Family Life

A Cotswold Family Life

Clare Mackintosh

SPHERE

First published in Great Britain in 2019 by Sphere
1 3 5 7 9 10 8 6 4 2

A CIP catalogue record for this book is available from the British Library.

ISBN 978-0-7515-7557-6

Typeset in Sabon by Palimpsest Book Production Limited, Falkirk, Stirlingshire
Printed and bound in Great Britain by Clays Ltd, Elcograf S.p.A.

Papers used by Sphere are from well-managed forests and other responsible sources.

MIX
Paper from
responsible sources
FSC
www.fsc.org
FSC® C104740

Sphere
An imprint of
Little, Brown Book Group
Carmelite House
50 Victoria Embankment
London EC4Y 0DZ

An Hachette UK Company
www.hachette.co.uk

www.littlebrown.co.uk

For Josh, Evie and George

Contents

Introduction

I have always loved the Cotswolds. I think I loved them even before I found them, in that half-formed vision one has of where to put down roots. Somewhere peaceful and green, where the road meanders between drystone walls and from village to village, and a strip of blue bursts from brook to river and back again.

In 2005 my husband Rob and I started house-hunting, spending weeks exploring towns and villages, before finally finding a place in which to hang our hats. Chipping Norton in Oxfordshire – known as the gateway to the Cotswolds, and just as honeyed as its Gloucestershire siblings – had a bustling high street, a theatre, a bookshop. Being there felt like a holiday, yet at the same time it felt like home.

That same year I left my job as a detective in Oxford CID, to take up promotion as Chipping Norton's town sergeant, thereby turning my life into one long episode of *Heartbeat*. Townsfolk arrived at our front door with lost property, caught me in the Co-op queue with complaints about parking, and dropped off braces of pheasants with a nod and a wink. I developed the necessary knack of turning a blind eye to minor transgressions and pub lock-ins, and reaped the benefits at times when failing police resources meant the locals were my only back-up.

I joined the police when I was twenty-three, setting aside my long-held ambitions to work in the arts. As a child, I had longed to be a performer, spending all my free time on stage or at dance classes. In my teens, I wrote terrible poetry, and short, pithy observations on life, writings that were hidden in notebooks and never shared. As I walked the thin blue line, never writing anything more creative than an overtime claim, I felt something wither inside me. I made vain attempts to spice up the statements I took from the victims of crime. 'Are you sure the suspect was just *walking*?' I'd say. 'Could he perhaps have been *limping*? Or *shuffling*? How about *pacing towards you in a menacing way*?' My witness would look at me blankly, and I would finish writing up the statement, sighing inwardly at its pedestrian tones.

Feeling stifled by my collar and tie, I started writing again, this time at home, stuffing scraps of paper into my bedside table like a guilty secret. Snatches of story, angry commentary, flashes of personal reflection on something and nothing. I wrote and I wrote, and each sentence peeled me a fraction more away from the day job. Craving an outlet, I sought refuge online, blogging anonymously about bad parenting, interrupted sex and emotional angst, and gradually my blog – More than just a Mother, as it was then – gained a following. Such a following, in fact, that the editor of *Cotswold Life* magazine offered me a column.

'What's your name?' he asked.

I panicked. I had, by then, left my job in Chipping Norton,

and become a police inspector, responsible for policing public events across Oxfordshire. I had profile. Responsibility. A really-rather-intimidating Chief Constable. What would it do to my credibility as a public order commander, to ponder in print about the time I inadvertently carried a dirty nappy to work in my handbag?

And so 'Emily Carlisle' was born. A name plucked from nowhere, with the help of Rob, who found the whole thing rather fun. Soon, that *Cotswold Life* column resulted in commissions for articles in magazines and newspapers, and I gradually acquired an accidental second job as a pseudo-journalist.

I grew rather fond of Emily. She was far more adventurous than I was; audacious and confident, witty and sharp. The children – Josh, Evie and George – grew used to my being called Emily on press trips, and even Rob stopped raising his eyebrows as he took another phone message for her. (Secretly, I think he liked Emily too: sleeping with two women added a certain frisson to his life, without the headache of an affair.)

Back in the day job, the pressure was mounting. Chief Inspector boards were looming, and as part of my preparation for the rank I took part in what was known as a 360-degree assessment. Feedback forms were sent to a selection of colleagues at every rank, with the aim of producing an accurate picture of my performance. It is a process every bit as ghastly as it sounds, but the end result was – and please forgive my immodesty – really rather good. I was *unfailingly cheerful*. My door was *always open*, and I *made time for everyone*. I was *optimistic* and *thoughtful*;

considerate and *kind*; *professional* and *extremely competent*. In short, I was good at my job.

I was thrilled. I took the report home to show Rob, who read it thoughtfully. 'This is great,' he said. 'But who's this woman? I don't think I know her . . .'

It was, as the cliché runs, a wake-up call. As many others had done before me, I had been saving all the best bits of me for work and leaving my family the leftovers. I was not *unfailingly cheerful* at home. I was not *optimistic* or *thoughtful*. And anyone witnessing me trying to put three toddlers to bed would confirm that I was neither *professional*, nor *extremely competent*.

Something had to give, and it wasn't going to be my family. In 2011 I left the police to work from home as a freelance copywriter and journalist, abandoning Emily Carlisle to write under my own name. I started work on a book. That book became *I Let You Go*, which sold more than a million copies, and turned me into a full-time novelist who still has to pinch herself most mornings.

I couldn't have left the police without the income freelance writing gave me, and I wouldn't have had that freelance career without that offer of a column in *Cotswold Life*; and so this book brings my career full circle. It has been a joy to revisit the many columns I have written over the years, to weave them into a story of family life, and to do so against the ever-changing – yet ever-lovely – backdrop of the Cotswolds.

Rob and I arrived in Chipping Norton as newly-weds. A decade later, we had three children and our lives were filled with friends and committees and commitments.

Much changes in a family during ten years, and the writing that follows charts many of those transformations. Jobs changed, pets came and went, and the children grew from toddlers to almost-teens. I have blurred the edges of these stories a little to allow columns that were intended to be read month by month, to become one complete tale. The tale of an ordinary family, doing ordinary things, in an area that is anything but ordinary.

Perhaps you know the Cotswolds intimately; perhaps you've never visited. Either way, I hope that *A Cotswold Family Life* gives you a window into a world filled with buttery stone and rolling hills, and with gloriously insane traditions such as cheese-rolling and onion-eating competitions. I hope it gives you a window into my life as a mother and a writer.

Above all, I hope you enjoy it.

JANUARY

January brings the snow,
Makes our feet and fingers glow.

Sara Coleridge

There is a sluggishness about January that only exists indoors, where the fridge still groans with turkey that won't be eaten, and stilton that shouldn't be but will be. The children are fractious and spoilt, the adults little better, and no one knows what day it is, or when anyone's back at work. Everything has finished. Fun has flatlined.

It is hard, amid these post-Christmas blues, to force yourself out of a toasty house (and doubly hard to convince the children to leave their new Lego and Rubik's Cubes and PlayStations) yet you persist, because you know it will make everything better. You know that the bickering will cease, and the lethargy will lift, and that everyone will be glad – in the end – that you went out.

Bundled up in coats and scarves, lost gloves found and wellies donned, you shepherd complaining troops through the door. You listen to the grumbles, and you referee the squabbles, and you hold hands and cross roads, and you head for the hills.

And there, the magic happens.

There, with the cold misting your breath, and the tramping of boots on frozen fields, spirits begin to lift. Because how could they not, when spiders' webs sparkle as though they've been dipped in glitter, and hoar frosts coat the trees so you have to look twice to check it isn't snow? How could smiles stay hidden, when the fieldfare are hopping so purposefully across the meadows, looking every inch like serious businessmen in grey bowler hats? And, as you reach the top of the hill, how could anyone squabble when the mist in the valley covers the folds of the hills like it's keeping a secret?

The woodlands are carpeted with sweet-chestnut casings that crunch beneath your feet, and the hedgerows hide hawthorn berries and rosehips, ripe for the jellies and jams you always mean to make yet never quite get round to. And it doesn't matter – because they'll be there next January, and the January after that, and one year you will have time. You can't see the bulbs, but you know they are there – that the promise of snowdrops and crocuses and bluebells lies just beneath the ground, waiting for their moment.

You walk for a mile, although nobody's counting, and when you return from the fields with your troops the glow in their cheeks is mirrored in yours. There is stamping of feet and blowing of hands, and the promise of hot chocolate with marshmallows and cream. The cobwebs have been blown away, and – for a while, at least – the arguments have stopped.

Now January feels like the start of something, and not the end.

Now, like the fields, the year feels full of promise.

Volume control

I don't like New Year's resolutions. Never have done. Life is hectic enough without the added pressure of a promise made to myself under the influence of a few too many glasses of Chablis, drunkenly shared with anyone in earshot.

Not that anyone really listens; for all the chit-chat at the pre-midnight dinner, nobody gives two hoots about your New Year's resolution. No one *really* wants to hear what you're pledging to give up this year, because quite apart from the fact that they all know you'll have abandoned your good intentions by Valentine's Day, the fact of the matter is that one resolution sounds very much like another. If your elderly neighbour announced his intention to stop smoking crack, or Eileen from the PTA confided her plans to quit the swinging parties with Derek and Angela from number 43, now *that* would be worth listening to. But it's never that interesting. It's just the same old, same old resolutions.

Well, here's what I *won't* be giving up this year.

I won't be giving up smoking. That particular vice was consigned to the sin bin when I fell pregnant, to be resurrected only at times when I'm feeling particularly naughty. Which isn't often.

I could give up illegal drugs, but I'd have to start taking them first. I can't give up drinking; I have three children – how else am I expected to get through bedtime?

I flatly refuse to give up eating. Diets just aren't for me. No bread? No cupcakes? No left-over fish fingers hoovered up from the children's plates and washed down with sugary tea? No siree. Despite getting perilously close to a time when I can no longer lay claim to having baby weight, I have no intention to live off rice cakes and carrot sticks.

Exercise is the obvious one. I used to be quite fit, once upon a time. In fact, I once ran a 10k without abject humiliation. Now I get out of breath just contemplating a run, and my gym gear lies sweating in a plastic bag. My stomach muscles haven't just separated – they're filing for divorce.

But vowing to get fit is simply the dullest New Year's resolution going – surely I can be more original than that?

I could learn a skill, that's quite popular at this time of year. But I already know how to cook, and I'm a dab hand at crafts, and I speak fluent French and passable German. The local adult education centre doesn't offer much more than that, except for computer programming, which is full of men called Colin with shiny trousers and dubious personal hygiene.

Could I resolve to do more for the community? Visit the elderly perhaps, or litter-pick once a week with the town council? But my committee tally already sits at six, and my husband complains he never sees me, so any resolution I make should be capable of being fulfilled within the confines of the home.

Housework? Oh pur-lease. Who was it who said 'dull women have immaculate houses'? Suffice to say, if you saw the state of my house you would have no hesitation in concluding that I must be A Lot of Fun.

That only leaves motherhood. I could resolve to be better at motherhood. What's that, I hear you cry? I'm a prime example of the perfect mother?

Cough.

Never mind the Yummy Mummies, the Slummy Mummies and the Tiger Moms: meet Shouty Mummy. Despite my best intentions, barely an hour into the day I find myself bellowing at the children to *get dressed, eat faster, tidy up, sit down, stand up* . . . I just can't help myself. Oh, the irony, when I catch myself screaming at the children to 'STOP SHOUTING!' It has to cease.

And so my resolution for this year is a simple one: to stop shouting at the children, who are not at this time deaf, but may well be if I carry on making such a racket.

I'll let you know how I get on.

Quietly.

Lay a little egg for me

Once the preserve of smallholders and farmers' wives, chicken-keeping has become quite the housewife's choice. As ubiquitous as the Emma Bridgewater pottery and the Cath Kidston tea towels that punctuate Cotswold kitchens, hen houses provide the full stop at the bottom of gardens across the region.

Have I succumbed to this trend? Oh of course I have, I'm a Cotswold mother. But first I had to battle it out with Rob, who was not convinced that we needed any livestock beyond the three children. 'Just think of the money we'll save on eggs!' I wheedled, tempting him with promises of home-baked brownies, freshly scrambled breakfasts and hard-boiled lunches.

I waved my pristine poultry-keeping book in his face and quoted figures at him. 'Say half a dozen eggs are £1.50 in the shops, and we'd get twenty-four eggs from four hens – because they'll probably want a day off – so that's six pounds a week we can save off our food bill – that's three hundred pounds a year! And the grain hardly costs anything, and they can have all our table scraps, so really they pay for themselves.'

I think he agreed just to stop me talking.

I hadn't factored in the initial outlay; the hen house cost nearly two hundred pounds. But it looked lovely on the lawn – and after all, the chickens had to live somewhere, didn't they? I painted the house cream and filled it with hens that proceeded to destroy the vegetable patch, tear up the grass and stain the patio with alarmingly frequent droppings.

Within a few weeks I had to face the facts. My charmingly bucolic vision of hens scratching round the back door was unworkable – we needed to build a run. A hundred pounds' worth of wood and wire later and the chickens were safely fenced at the end of the lawn, so we made a rather expensive trip to the garden centre to replace the plants ravaged by our new pets. I mentally totted up what they'd cost us to date. Okay, so it was going to take a little longer than I thought before we broke even, but we'd get there. Eventually.

But then we got red mite. From what I can gather, red mite are a little like head lice in a primary school. Pretty much unavoidable and a bugger to get rid of. I scoured the internet for solutions, scrubbing the hen house with all manner of disinfectant and covering the hens in powder till they sneezed. Friends of friends proffered shady dealings in black-market creosote, and shook their heads knowingly when I declined. Within days the mite were back in their thousands.

I admitted defeat.

I sought advice from the experts and nearly wept when I realised we had no choice but to burn my beautiful wooden hen house. As I watched the cream slats go up in flames, Rob came outside and assessed the extremely-ugly-but-immune-to-red-mite plastic house I'd had to buy that afternoon for a staggering three hundred pounds.

'So how much do you think these chickens have cost us in their first year?' he enquired mildly.

I winced, having already done the sums. 'About seven hundred pounds,' I muttered.

He thought for a while. 'So they still owe us four hundred?' I threw another piece of infested wood onto my impromptu bonfire and decided not to answer.

'Still,' he said, more brightly, 'in a couple of years we should have made our money back and be making some real savings on all those eggs.' He paused as though he'd just thought of something. 'How long is it, again, before their egg production starts to slow down?'

I prodded the ashes savagely before giving him the answer he already knew. 'Two years.'

He nodded thoughtfully and made his way back to the house.

I think I'll leave it a while before I suggest we try our hand at raising pigs.

Building blocks

We have the builders in. They've been in for so long I can scarcely remember a time when they were out. The estimated date of completion has been and gone, and now I am resigned to their presence in the same way that I suffer traffic wardens, or flies on a summer picnic.

When they first started, weeks ago now, I made sure I was up and dressed before they arrived. It was an effort that fast became exhausting, particularly on weekdays, when shooing three children into uniforms and out of the door is already quite a feat, even without the distractions of builders.

Now I find myself disturbingly blasé about our part-time houseguests, who are equally (and slightly insultingly) unmoved by the sight of my pyjama-clad figure wandering into the kitchen. They nod a greeting, then stare meaningfully at the kettle, which – despite several invitations – they seem to be incapable of lifting themselves.

I have made more cups of tea and coffee for other people in the last six weeks than it would be possible to drink myself in my entire lifetime. White with one, white with two, black with three . . . I know everyone's preferences as well as the office intern knows her colleagues'

Starbucks orders, and I'm able to muster about as much enthusiasm for the task.

When I'm not making tea, I'm answering questions. 'Yes, I'd like that handle there'; 'no, about three inches to the left'; 'horizontally, with a gap at the end'. It's all very taxing. Just as I get stuck in to whatever I'm writing, I'll hear a call from downstairs, where my presence is required for something that couldn't possibly wait.

'Cheers,' he'll say when I've made my executive decision, before nodding in the direction of the kettle. 'Don't s'pose there's any chance . . .?'

It is impossible to write against a backdrop of power tools and the occasional swear word as someone falls off a roof, and what with all the tea-making my productivity has taken a nosedive in recent weeks. Adding a certain frisson to my freelancing is the frequency with which the power is turned off without notice. Can I risk writing for two minutes between saves? Ten? Will that perfectly crafted sentence survive, or be lost for ever? With depressing inevitability it is always when I am in full flow that the computer goes off, my screen fading to a pinprick as the builder calls up the stairs to say he's 'just turned it off for a couple of minutes'.

'Right,' I mutter between clenched teeth, hoping to somehow hold on to the inspiration I felt just a moment ago.

'The downstairs circuit's still on, though,' he adds, 'if you want to put the kettle on . . .'

The first couple of weeks were a novelty. We camped out in the playroom, creating a temporary kitchen on the dining table and eating suppers of toast and tinned sardines balanced on our knees. The fun waned fast: nothing is where it should be, and not a single room has escaped the contents of what used to be our garage and will soon become our kitchen. There are golf clubs and wellies in the sitting room, piles of tools and paint tins in the play-room, and outdoor coats stuffed into the children's wardrobes. I have no idea where it is going to go once this is all over.

Amongst all the chaos I have fiercely guarded my cubby-hole of an office, refusing to allow the clutter to creep into the only space I consider to be all mine. But even here it's impossible to forget about the building work, thanks to the all-pervading dust that floats invisibly around the house before settling into each nook and cranny. Every room is covered in a light film of beige dust, and no matter how often I clean it just comes back. There is dust on the toilet roll in the downstairs loo, on every floor and every piece of furniture, and in inexplicable places, such as my handbag and the inside of my sock drawer.

There is dust everywhere, except, of course, on the kettle, which is never still for long enough to get grubby. Cup of tea, you say? How do you have it?

The confidence trick

At the leisure centre last week, as I waited for yet another child to finish yet another after-school activity, I got chatting to a gawky adolescent waiting for his sister. He was sixteen, perhaps seventeen, all elbows and spots and an invisible moustache he stroked from time to time.

'I'm going to audition for *Britain's Got Talent*,' he confided. 'I'm thinking of singing that one Ronan Keating does.'

I wished him luck. 'Maybe you could give *X-Factor* a go too.'

'Oh I will,' he said. 'At least, I will if I don't win *Britain's Got Talent*.'

Where does it come from, this unmitigated self-assurance? This confidence that the world is not only one's oyster, but a veritable ocean of opportunities, each wave bigger than the one before. Where does it come from? And more importantly, where does it go? How does the buoyancy of youth morph into the uncertainty of middle age, crippled with insecurities?

I know dozens of mothers. Hordes of women my age, with two or three children under their belt – and their feet – and a wealth of experience in the business arena.

These are women well used to running teams, managing conflict and solving problems. Women who can bring projects in on time and under budget. Women who, after a year or so with nothing more complex to address than a multi-buy wipes offer and a timetable clash between Tumble Tots and Water Babies, won't put themselves forward because they don't believe they can do it.

The reality is that they are just as capable as they ever were, they just don't think they are. I don't know what happens in that delivery suite, but I suspect midwives are hoiking out far more than a seven-pound baby. Self-esteem? Gone. Confidence? Gone. Ability to stay dry-eyed when the Andrex advert airs? Gone. Whipped away and out with the medical waste while you're still distracted by the new arrival.

Of course, all that leaves rather a big gap, so presumably they shove in a few new bits to fill the space: a heavy dose of guilt, an addiction to chocolate, and that extraordinary enhanced hearing ability which makes your gut twist every time a child cries 'Mummy!' within a three-mile radius.

I don't mind the extras, really I don't. The guilt reminds me what's important in life, and the chocolate addiction – well, I would probably be better off without that one.

But I would like my confidence back.

I miss it.

I had to clear out the loft the other day and I came across my university dissertation. I sat for ages, marvelling at the bold statements, the compelling arguments, the confident conclusion. Who was this girl who knew nothing about global economics, yet wrote so deftly about it? Where did she go?

I think the children are to blame, although I wouldn't have it any other way. I suspect that motherhood is a job so challenging, so all-consuming, that it sweeps us off our feet in a way that no boardroom role could do. When we succeed as mothers – as we all do, whatever we think at the time – we should be jubilant. We should be cock-a-hoop, brimming with confidence at our ability to overcome our toughest job yet.

Because our children are so small, and the world is so big, we feel so keenly the responsibility of preparing them for it, and we feel we have never quite done enough. We are never quite good enough.

It takes time to recognise that we have in fact achieved something incredible, something breath-taking. We feel inadequate, when the reality is that we are quite the reverse.

I shall remind myself of this fact next time I am required to 'sell' myself.

I am a mother. I am amazing.

I'm not sure about *Britain's Got Talent*, though. I think I might just sit that one out.

Puppy love

We're doing it again. Despite saying we never would, that life is so much easier now that we can go away when we like, and go out for the whole day at the drop of a hat, we're still going through it all again. We're going back to night-time wakings, early-morning crying and toilet-training, and turning our lives upside down.

We're getting a puppy.

I have for some time begged for a little addition to the family. I have waited patiently – well, I have waited – and now that the children are all at school and my hours less stretched, we are finally getting a dog, and she arrives this week.

Without a dog, there was something missing from my life as a Cotswold mother. I have the children. I have the Cath Kidston prints and the ironically cheerful wellies. I have the reusable shopping bags, the Joules dresses and the husband who works too much. But I don't have a dog. Recently I've felt positively bereft as I've walked with the children through the woods, my right hand trailing uselessly where it should be holding a lead, or reaching for treats to reward my loyal companion.

A proper Cotswold family needs a dog. We used to

have a black labrador (we are nothing if not predictable) but he bit one of the children and the situation demanded action. It was tough deciding which one should go – we really did like the dog, and he was toilet-trained, unlike Josh at the time – but eventually Toby was packed off to live in luxury with my mother-in-law in Burford, where he received far more attention than he ever would have done in a house with three children and four chickens.

But any hint from me that another dog would be lovely, now that I was at home all day and the children were so much older, was met with firm dismissal from Rob, who still maintains I coerced him into hen-keeping. Which is only partially true. Josh, who spent years terrified of anything on four legs since the dog-biting incident, made huge efforts to overcome his phobia with the help of some friends' trustworthy pets. He grew desperate for a dog of his own and thus I had a staunch ally in my Give the Cotswold Mother a Dog campaign. Evie and George were easily brought onside, which just left my husband in the anti-dog camp. In the face of this, I mounted a three-pronged attack.

First, the safety angle. Surely a dog would be good for security? After all, Rob works nights, leaving the children and me alone in the house – how could he deny me protection? Unfortunately this is tenuous: we live in one of the safest areas in Britain. A kicked-over bin makes headline news, and the members of the Neighbourhood Watch are so bored they've taken up knitting. I wondered if I could persuade some undesirables to carry out a small burglary. Nothing major – I'm quite fond of the family silver – just enough to provoke thought from my husband about how best to protect the house. And perhaps they could take some of the plastic crap from the playroom while they're at it.

The second arm of my campaign involved the children – a little emotional blackmail goes a long way, I find. A series of paintings now adorns the kitchen walls, featuring the children frolicking with a sweet dog of miscellaneous origin. The children got bored after the second one so I resorted to painting a dog into any family portrait they brought back from school. Subliminal messaging, I think they call it. I coached child number two (the cutest and most irresistible) to wail gently in a corner at strategic moments. When her concerned father approached and asked what was wrong, she was to turn up her tear-stained face and whisper 'If only I had a dog . . .'

But it was all taking too long. Time to bring out the big guns – a tried and tested method seen in households up and down the country. A wistful sigh as I flicked through old family photographs, a longing look at a friend's new baby, perhaps the impulse purchase of a pink Babygro, and the merest suggestion that *another baby would be nice*.

Rob was on the Kennel Club website faster than you can say vasectomy.

And really, it's a social obligation. Everyone I know has a dog. Sleek pedigrees with names like Mackenzie Mull of Mallaig, more paperwork than a bureaucrat and a coat gleaming with good health. Rescue dogs called Alfie, Champ and Digger, with furiously wagging tails and hopeful expressions. And then there's the new fashion for dogs like pugles, labradoodles and giant schnoodles – dogs that used to be called mongrels but are now trendy breeds.

Having been surrounded by so many four-legged companions, we've thought long and hard about breeds. Several friends advised us to get a cockapoo: good with children, apparently, although that's not their only selling point.

'They don't shed!' their owners cry enthusiastically, as though offering the secret to eternal happiness. I admit that clearing drifts of dog hair isn't the most appealing prospect, but to choose a dog based on the effect it has on your household chores? It's a little too Stepford for my liking.

Then, of course, we had to choose a name. I regretted my attempt to foster a sense of democracy, when the children's collective brainstorm produced a shortlist of Winner, Dog, and Fluffy.

'We can't call her Winner,' I said, 'it's too much to live up to. We'll give her an inferiority complex.'

'Well, I'm not standing at the back door yelling "Fluffy!"' my husband proclaimed. He had a point.

'That just leaves Dog, then,' I said.

Sod democracy.

We decided on Maddie, a pretty name I rather wish I had used for one of the children. She's a springer spaniel. Yes, a springer. You don't have to tell me, I know they're bonkers. And in case I wasn't already aware, there have been no shortage of reminders. Rather like when you're pregnant ('*Definitely a "boy" bump*', '*You are going to breast-feed, aren't you?*' '*Routine is the key!*'), as soon as you mention you're getting a dog, people consider it their born right to offer unwanted advice on everything from breed choice to training tips. I was led to believe that Britain was a nation of dog-lovers, but you would never know it, to listen to the litany of horror stories that has followed me around since I announced our decision to get a dog.

Vet bills that cause bankruptcy, dogs who destroy entire sofas, dogs who terrorise villages, bite children and worry sheep. It seems everyone has a cautionary tale to tell about owning a dog. Where are the *happy* dog owners? There must be some. Even as an expectant mother there were occasional flashes of parental pride in amongst the stories of cracked nipples and crayoned walls.

I can't wait for Maddie to arrive. I sit all day in my little home office, with nothing to distract me but a computer screen and a tin of biscuits. I eat too much and walk too little. I tweet instead of talking and I spend too much time indoors. Having a dog will change things. I can't wait to turn right instead of left after I drop off the children, and march through the fields with someone who won't expect answers to questions that don't make sense. I'm looking forward to taking her to training classes, and to playing Barbara Woodhouse. I may even start wearing headscarves. It's going to be great.

Of course, she'll be bonkers. Of course she'll cost me a fortune in vet bills and chewed shoes. But you know what? The children are a bit bonkers too. They jump on the furniture and they 'accidentally' carve their names in the kitchen table. They force me out to stand in a freezing cold park when I'd rather be curled up with a book and a mug of hot chocolate. They tramp mud all over the house, create mountains of washing and occasionally – just occasionally – you might hear me mutter something about why on earth I had children anyway.

But I wouldn't have it any other way.

Morning has broken

The school has launched a punctuality drive. It's not their fault: the council has descended on them like a ton of textbooks, threatening all manner of sanctions if the situation doesn't improve. Targets have been set, stern letters sent home, and the children bribed with certificates of attendance if they hit the magic 98 per cent. Yesterday George came home empty-handed and with glistening eyes, as the other two triumphantly waved pieces of gold paper.

'But I was poorly!' The wail was fuelled by the frustration of injustice.

They have all been ill – sick bugs rarely discriminate as they sweep through a family – but George's bouts fell squarely mid-week, while the others succumbed at weekends. I began to try to justify the lack of certificate to my sobbing child, but failed.

Because actually it simply *wasn't* fair.

What's a parent supposed to do – send a vomiting child into school? Ignore the streaming cold and let them pass it round the class? Of course not. So to penalise a parent – and trust me, placating a child who has missed out on a certificate printed on gold paper is indeed a penalty – for taking good care of ailing children seems a little harsh.

When I was in the police force a scheme was introduced whereby a 100 per cent attendance record resulted in a hundred-pound bonus at Christmas. It didn't last long, but while it did, hundreds of police officers and support staff coughed and spluttered their way through meetings, dragging themselves into work despite raging temperatures and broken legs, in order to claim their bonus. One colleague of mine began mainlining vitamin supplements and herbal energy products, until he realised he was spending more on trying to maintain his health than he would recoup in reward.

Of course I want my children to be in school as much as possible. In fact, if you've ever seen the way they behave at the weekend, you would understand my absolute enthusiasm for this. So if I can't do anything about the days off sick – short of pushing fruit and veg on them with the enthusiasm of a back-alley crack dealer – I can at least make sure they are punctual the rest of the time.

Easier said than done.

The school bus leaves from the top of our hill (for 'hill', read 'near-vertical climb') at 8.45 a.m., which means we need to be out of the door by 8.35 a.m. on the dot. Every day. I know this – it's a routine we have now had for two years. Yet every single morning, 8.35 a.m. sees me frantically pulling on jeans and drying my hair simultaneously, while shouting at the children to get-the-lunches-out-of-the-fridge-and-put-your-coats-on-and-can-someone-please-find-my-keys?

I start with good intentions, at 7 a.m. when the alarm goes off and I open one eye to check I'm still alive. But somehow, instead of opening the other eye, I find myself snuggling back down under the duvet, snoozing my alarm with sloth-like prowess. Waking again at 7.45 a.m., I spend the next half-hour dragging three children out of bed and chasing them through the various activities they do every day, yet look at me with abject horror when asked to do them. 'What do you MEAN, I have to clean my TEETH?' 'You want me to put on SOCKS?' 'No, I haven't had breakfast – was I supposed to?'

When I think it is safe – the majority of essential tasks are complete, and the children are at least making a pretence of putting uniform on – I will jump in the shower, with time only for what my mother would call the important bits.

Despite the children now being old enough to dress themselves, I'm still liable to emerge from the shower to find Josh standing in the middle of his bedroom with nothing on but a pair of pants, and George locked in the bathroom with an alarming air of permanence.

'Just having a poo,' comes the explanation.

'THERE IS NO TIME FOR POOS!' I roar. 'THE MORNING ROUTINE DOES NOT ALLOW FOR POOS!'

And so, every morning, you will find me charging up the hill with three panting children, hoping against hope that the bus driver will wait just a couple of minutes for us.

It is clear that any punctuality problems involving my

children can be laid firmly at my door. Perhaps the school could introduce a reward scheme for me, with the promise of a prize if I make it out of the house on time for an entire term.

And a certificate – on gold paper, naturally.

It's just not tennis

According to an article I read recently, couples who play together, stay together. Ignoring the fact that advice from self-styled relationship experts generally makes me nauseous, I wondered if it might be true.

Perhaps Rob and I should take up a sport.

I have avoided suggesting it until now. The problem is that Rob is genetically athletic, and I have the grace and coordination of an arthritic hippopotamus. A reluctant member of my high-school netball team, I took my goose pimples off to the sidelines at the earliest opportunity, much to the relief of my leggy compatriots. Since then, an avalanche of children has sapped me of the ability to run without crashing into something or tripping over my own feet.

In stark comparison, Rob began kicking a rugby ball when he was practically still in the womb, played junior cricket for England and boasts an impressive golf handicap despite rarely getting his clubs out. It's all deeply irritating, as despite my lack of sporting prowess I am intensely competitive and a terrible loser who will reluctantly shake hands and mutter 'well done' through gritted teeth.

I'd like to say I could outwit him in more cerebral

pastimes, to make up for continually being thrashed on the sports field, but he has encyclopaedic general knowledge and the memory of an elephant. We were once on the same team in a three-hour game of after-dinner Trivial Pursuit, during which my sole contribution was rolling the die and lining up our team's wedges in rainbow order. I blame the fact that the edition was from 1983, which meant that every answer had to preclude the historical context added by the last twenty-eight years. Frankly I have enough trouble correctly guessing where the town of Sassnitz is (I thought it was Russia), without also having to remember that the Berlin Wall was still up in the 80s.

Anyway, far better to do something more active together. I briefly considered bowls, but the knee-length skirts are so unflattering, and Rob vetoed it on the basis that we are, after all, still in our forties. Darts struck me as inherently dangerous for those around me, and bending over a snooker table best avoided, given those child-bearing hips of mine.

I eventually plumped for tennis, after quizzing Rob about when he last played. 'Gosh, not for twenty years or so,' he said. 'I'm not sure I can remember how.'

Perfect.

I booked the court and dug out a dubious pair of shorts I once used for painting the shed. They made me feel really rather sporty, and I jogged optimistically onto the court, only to see Rob adopt an alarmingly professional stance, before pocketing a spare ball and launching the other towards me at full pelt.

I lunged to my right with a suitable grunt but the ball

appeared to sail clean through my racket. I examined the strings for holes but nothing seemed obvious.

'Keep your eye on the ball,' Rob suggested helpfully. I shot him a withering look but it was interrupted by another missile hurtling towards me. I ducked. It seemed like the sensible thing to do.

Twenty minutes later I had failed to make contact with a single ball, and stormed off the court in a fit of pique when Rob snorted with laughter at my attempts to serve.

It didn't bode well, and I was rather concerned that this inability to play games together was the death knell of our relationship. I wonder if it is better to play together and argue about it, or not to play together at all? If I persist with the advice of the relationship experts, we could be in for years of competitive angst, culminating in a silent round of Scrabble where one of us spells out D-I-V-O-R-C-E on a triple word score (thirty-nine points).

Come to think of it, I was always rather good at Scrabble. Maybe we'll give game-playing just one more shot . . .

Stocking up for winter

I'm a big fan of online grocery shopping. Any activity I can do in my pyjamas whilst watching *EastEnders* gets my vote, and sadly there are far fewer of those now that we've taken the television out of our bedroom.

Unfortunately sometimes the cupboards are so bare I can't wait for the delivery van, unless I want to explain to Social Services why the children are living off chicken feed and butter, both of which we always seem to have in abundance.

Reluctantly I visited my local supermarket on Saturday to stock up on essentials, only to be greeted by post-apocalyptic shelves and a dozen half-crazed women fighting over bottled water. Snow was clearly heading our way again. The supermarkets are always mobbed as soon as the forecast gets bad; it's terribly predictable. In fact I suspect I could do without a weather report altogether, instead forming an accurate assessment on the basis of the Co-op's bread aisle. On this occasion I decided against fighting over the last baguette (I got there first, but my opponent had a gimlet stare and a steely grip that could crack walnuts), heading home with my dignity intact and my shopping bags decidedly empty.

Back in the kitchen I wondered how we'd fare if bad weather did actually set in, and we had to make do for a week or so. Or perhaps longer – maybe that woman with the trolleyload of beans had insider information. I should have watched to see what else she was stockpiling. We are regularly snowed in each January, yet I am just as regularly woefully underprepared. Last year the children had no waterproof trousers, so with eight inches of snow and legs only a little longer, we were housebound for a fortnight. This year the children are properly equipped for a Cotswold ski fest, and all that is left is to plan our provisions.

I pulled open the larder door and perused its contents. The larder is voluminous and rammed to the gunnels, and at first glance you might think it appears well-stocked, but on closer inspection it doesn't actually seem to hold anything useful.

Why do I have so much treacle? I'm not even sure I know what to do with treacle. And three tubs of bicarbonate of soda? I counted seven packets of jelly and four of Angel Delight, two empty cereal packets and a mouse trap. It seemed our larder didn't hold anything we could actually *eat*.

My *Living the Good Life* book suggested we might store root vegetables harvested at the end of the summer to carry us through the winter. Delicious though they were, it didn't seem worth packing our seven carrots into sandboxes, and they were eaten in a week.

I shared my concerns with Rob, who seemed relatively indifferent about the matter.

'We'd just eat one of the chickens,' was his suggestion. I was outraged – how could he be so callous? The chickens have dutifully provided us with breakfast, lashings of superb manure and an immeasurable amount of feel-good factor. They are surely as much a part of the family as the children themselves, and considerably less effort.

'Which one would you eat?' I asked, curious in spite of myself. We surveyed the chooks as they roamed around the frozen garden. Mrs Greedy doesn't have a scrap of meat on her, but Princess Layer is positively ripe for the roasting tin. Great chunky thighs and a large plump breast nestle beneath golden feathers. She caught us salivating and retreated behind the compost heap as if she could read minds.

'So could you actually – you know?' I checked that the chickens weren't looking and mimed a sort of poultry-throttling motion.

'Of course I could.' My husband appears to have rein-vented himself as Bear Grylls. Any day now I'll find him crouched in the sitting room whittling a weapon and drinking his own urine. 'If we were starving.'

'So if we got snowed in today,' I said, 'with just the food we've got in our cupboards – how long before you'd kill a chicken for me?' I was keen to establish just how hungry I'd need to be before my hunter-gatherer spouse sharpened his axe. Just a bit peckish? Or positively weak with exhaustion, fingers barely able to pluck out the feathers before slathering Princess Layer with butter and poking an onion up her bottom?

'If the children were hungry,' he said nobly, 'I would

find them food.' He looked around the garden as though bursting from the undergrowth were armfuls of edible flora and fauna, instead of a dozen tennis balls and a rusty bucket.

Treacle on toast it is, then.

FEBRUARY

Late February days; and now, at last,
Might you have thought that winter's woe was past;
So fair the sky was, and so soft the air.

William Morris

If January holds promise for the year ahead, February too often seems to have snatched it away. Sunlight hides beneath grey skies and ever-present rain, and darkness bookends too-short days.

But February is the frontier between winter and spring, and there is always at least one day that hints at what will soon be here. Snowdrops, pushing through woodland floors, starkly white and always, but always, taking you by surprise, like Narnia's thaw when Aslan appears. *Winter meets its death.*

You spot tiny stars of chickweed, creeping around the edges of the supermarket car park. You see a flash of blue iris on your drive back home. And when the rain holds off, and the dog begs you for a walk, you find you can grab bunches of wild garlic leaves, for the quickest pesto pasta, because once again you shopped without a list, and now you have nothing that will actually make a meal. You look around with newly opened eyes, and you see the barely-there buds on the trees; the tint of green where just a week ago there had been only brown.

If you listen hard, you'll hear a mistle thrush start and then stop abruptly, as though interrupted by the tap-tap-tap of a nuthatch on its tree elsewhere in the garden. *Start stop. Start stop.* Chaffinches and blue tits will cling to the ball you made from beef suet and bird seed in a rash moment of domestic perfection, and you'll feel absurdly happy to have made a difference. You'll remember to put out water, too, and you'll read an article about shelter for garden insects and smugly pretend you left all those autumn leaves there deliberately.

You might even catch a glimpse of roe deer, skirting still-frosty fields beside leafless hedges; far too flighty for a camera phone, yet majestic enough for you to text somebody – anybody – *guess what I just saw in the field!*

February takes its name from the Latin *februum*, meaning purification, and it is a good month for abstinence. Not quite winter, yet not quite spring, it is a month for soup suppers and early nights; for board games and television dramas. It is a month for making plans you're not quite ready to start, and talking over a bottle of wine about what you'll do *when the evenings get longer.* It is a month for hunkering down and feeding the woodburner with logs from the dwindling pile in the shed you thought would last you all winter.

It is a month (as you will constantly remind yourself) that is blissfully, mercifully, short.

Listen with Mother

My heart filled with joy the first time one of my children asked to read their school book to themselves, instead of reading aloud to me. Not (just) because it was an indication of how far they had come, and not (just) because it meant I could instead make packed lunches, locate a lost pair of trainers, and work out how to magic some supper out of a packet of bacon, a tin of chickpeas and some leftover roast potatoes. No, my buoyant mood stemmed instead from the sheer relief that I no longer had to sit at the kitchen table, listening to a child stammer their way through the Magic Key series.

I love being with my children. I love reading. Ergo, I should love listening to my children read, right?

Not so.

I take my hat off to primary school teachers, because listening to a non-fluent reader makes me want to rip my own ears off and use them as bookmarks.

'Sound it out,' I'd say to a then six-year-old Evie.

'K–i–t–t–e–n,' she'd say confidently.

'Brilliant!' I'd cheer. 'So what's the word?'

A moment's silence, as she'd scan the illustrations hopefully. 'Cat?'

'Not quite!' I'd trill through gritted teeth. 'Let's try again.' On and on it would go, my jaw spasming from engineered smiling.

With three children, all born within fifteen months, evening reading was a production-line affair. Twins Evie and George first, then their older brother, Josh's seniority meaning chapters instead of pictures – books an inch thick instead of pamphlet-thin. Even then I struggled.

'Oh. No. Cried. Mum,' Josh would intone, the most exciting story rendered dull as ditchwater by his laboured diction.

'Oh no!' I'd repeat, leaping up with an expression more fitting of a Hammer horror film. 'Hear the difference? Read that bit again.'

'Oh. No. Cried. Mum.'

I was beginning to know how she felt.

I am not blessed with patience. In this respect I am very much like my father, who drew huge pleasure from carrying out science experiments with his older grand-children, but never knew quite what to do with a toddler. Not for me the baby days, or the faltering steps of an almost-walker. Sweet? Yes. Amazing? Yes. Interesting? Not so much.

And so it is with reading. After that first term at school, when their transition from non-reader to reader seemed like alchemy, I found the reading journey more chore than pleasure. A necessary path to follow in pursuit of fluency.

But when they got there . . . oh what a joy!

Finally I could listen to their reading without a fortifying swig of Pinot Grigio, without straining to hear the words or make sense of a sentence lacking audible punctuation. Finally I could see the results of my Hammer-horror acting. My children looked up as they read, they smiled, they laughed, they used pauses to build suspense.

They were storytellers.

Now that my children are older, I am no longer obliged to sign their reading record beneath a suitably enthusiastic comment. Their reading is 'self-guided'; they choose their own books, read every day, and write a line or two about each story for their teacher to review. They are confident, articulate readers with eclectic literary tastes and a vocabulary to match.

'Will you read to me?' I asked Josh the other day.

He looked up from his book and smiled politely. 'I'd rather read in my head,' he told me. 'If you don't mind.'

But I did.

I remembered those after-school reading sessions, the chores neglected in favour of books. I remembered the rare opportunity they gave me to spend time with just one of my children. I remembered the weight of a small body in my lap, and the tickle of their hair on my cheek as I leaned forward to see the page.

I remembered it all. And I missed it.

Be my valentine

Even the most confirmed of bachelors couldn't fail to notice that Valentine's Day is in the offing. The shops are heaving with pink, and Hallmark has added still more categories to their personalised card range. Now you can declare your love to your boyfriend, girlfriend, spouse, parents, kids, grandchildren . . . probably even the babysitter, your second cousin twice removed, and that bloke who washes your car while you do the weekly shop.

Despite my cynicism about such commercialism, I have duly bought a card for my husband, which will sit alongside his offering to me for a week or two, before they go in the bin.

Although manufactured, the experts would have us believe that such scheduled romance is the key to a successful long-term relationship. Apparently, in order to allocate as much importance to our relationships as to our jobs, we should give them equal status in our calendars. If you feel like two ships passing in the night, the advice du jour is to pop a 'date night' in the diary. Never seem to get around to having sex? Schedule it for a week on Wednesday.

Shudder.

Is there anything less likely to get you in the mood than the knowledge that, regardless of how shitty your day's been, how knackered you are, or how much good telly there is on, you'll have to find the energy to swing from the chandeliers? What if you just don't feel like it – are you supposed to go ahead and do it anyway? How is that romantic?

Putting an end to courting was precisely why I got married in the first place. Who wants to return to the game-playing of dating, and risk breaking one of the myriad unwritten rules? I have a husband, not a boyfriend. I no longer have to be driven to a fixed-price-menu restaurant in a Fiat Punto, to have a glass of cheap wine and a bolognese before bumping noses over the goodbye and wondering if suggesting coffee means I'm easy. Nor do I need to agonise over precisely how long to leave it before calling to say thank you, or pluck up the courage to suggest another date.

From what I can glean from the advice columns, marital date nights mean some kind of odd role play, where he rings me from work – or perhaps just from downstairs – to ask me out, and I simper and pretend to check my calendar, even though we've had the day circled for the three months it took to arrange a babysitter. I'd have to fish in the laundry bin for a matching bra and pants, shave my legs, brush my hair . . . it's all such a lot of effort, when we could save the cost of the sitter and splurge on a takeaway to eat in our pyjamas. And let's face it, no matter how much you promise each other you're not going to talk about the children, it's rare to get beyond the aperitif without one of you caving and discussing little Johnnie's school report, or what on earth you're going to do about Harriet's tantrums.

Back when you were dating for real, conversation was easy: where you grew up, what music you liked, what countries you wanted to visit . . . You know all that stuff now. There's nothing left. So you whip through the kids, the place you'd buy if you could afford to move, all the jobs around the house you haven't finished yet, and by the main course you've run out of ideas and start discussing all the other couples in the restaurant. Who are all discussing you.

For the last six weeks, the shops have been rammed with cutesy teddy bears clutching red satin hearts, impaled upon racks of cards. We're encouraged to browse by genre ('Arty', 'Humorous', 'For My Wife') but I can't help thinking it would be more effective to display them under relationship-length categories instead. Surely it would speed up the buying process no end, if one knew exactly where to look?

At one end of the spectrum they could have a small selection of 'You Haven't Got a Hope in Hell' cards, for the bearded IT geeks swooning over the girl in accounts who wears the invisible skirt and can't work the photocopier. That range would be paired with cards suitable for 'Could Be in with a Chance if You Play Your Cards Right'.

Moving down the aisle you'd come to 'Still Counting the Relationship in Weeks', when things could go either way and you don't want to burn your bridges by coming on too strong with your Hallmark. An oh-so-amusing black and white card about an elephant breaking wind hits a nice light note for a fledgling relationship; the two-foot-tall gilt-embossed musical number with accompanying helium balloon and Steiff bear just screams stalker.

By the time you reach 'Six Months and Feeling Secure' you can probably risk a tentative heart or two, but for God's sake don't mention the L-word till you've been 'Together for a Whole Year'.

Fiancé cards are duty-bound to be nauseatingly romantic, but it's when you reach the 'Married' aisle that a whole raft of sub-categories is really needed. 'Newly-Weds' can still get away with the hearts and flowers, but by 'Five Years and Counting' the ardour has faded somewhat and it's back to the quips about breaking wind.

The 'Parents of Young Children' section can be pretty small. Let's face it, you're both so sleep-deprived that you could be handed a piece of folded up cereal packet and you wouldn't notice. 'Fifteen Years – You'd Get Less for Murder' would be a rather dull division; obviously no one's having sex any more, so no novelty handcuffs please – just some Shakespearian quotes and a tasteful reproduction of some eighteenth-century art.

At the far end of the aisle would sit the 'In It for the Long Haul' range, where anything goes in the way of cards and gifts because you're either a) steadfastly in love and likely to remain so, or b) resigned to the fact that it's better the devil you know.

For the past few years I have, without fail, received four

cards each Valentine's Day. One from each of my three children, lovingly smeared with Pritt Stick, glitter and unidentifiable bodily substances, and one from my husband, mercifully free from any of the above. Each year I linger hopefully by the letterbox, wondering if the postman will reveal I have a secret admirer. Not that I'm looking for extramarital distraction, you understand, but wouldn't it be exciting? An anonymous admirer, the only clue to his identity being the postmark, his handwriting and a predilection for Shakespearian quotes/teddy bears/jokes about elephants breaking wind. It hasn't happened yet. In fact, the last time I got a Valentine's card from someone I wasn't already in a relationship with, I was fourteen. I spent the rest of the term eyeing up likely candidates and stealing handwriting samples to compare with my by then dog-eared card. I never did find out who gave it to me.

I've sent a few anonymous cards myself over the years. I delivered several as a doe-eyed schoolgirl mooning about in the wake of testosterone-fuelled grammar school boys, daringly slipping cards into blazer pockets on the upper deck of the 280 bus. Nowadays I like to supplement my tasteful 'You're Not Perfect But You'll Do' card (delivered by hand with a cup of tea and a morning kiss) with the most garish Valentine's missive I can find (delivered anonymously via Royal Mail).

'Gosh, who could that be from?' I exclaim, my eyes widening in a performance worthy of an Oscar.

'I truly have no idea,' my ever-loving husband replies, only mildly exasperated by this annual pantomime. 'Someone with bad taste in cards, it would seem.'

Cards duly exchanged, I'll be watching out for the Interflora van just in case my so-secret-I've-never-seen-a-sign-of-him admirer decides to up the ante this year.

Happy Valentine's Day.

The space race

I am an expert at parking. I really am. Give me a tight space and a parallel-parking challenge, and I'll slip into it like an otter into water. It is a skill learned from my father and honed by years of attempting to walk as short a distance as possible with small children.

One busy Saturday I had to go to Oxford. Along with everyone else I ignored the 'car park full' sign at the entrance to the park and ride and orbited the packed tarmac in ever-depressing circles. There was nothing. A bus arrived and disgorged a pitiful handful of passengers, who were all immediately kerb-crawled back to their spaces by waiting cars. Eventually, right next to the buses, I came across a tiny space. A space so small that the other cars drove straight past it without a second glance. Perhaps they had dismissed it as unfeasibly small. Perhaps they hadn't seen it at all. Whatever the reason, it was all mine. I should point out at this stage that I don't drive a little car. I have a seven-seater people-carrier which is perfect for kids' play dates and being the designated driver on a girls' night out, but really isn't ideal for squeezing into tight spots. Nevertheless, I knew I could do it. I eased backwards, inch by inch, paying no heed to the frantic beeping of my parking sensors and slipping in carefully between a rather nice Jag and a filthy Fiesta. Victory! I half hoped for a round of applause, but none was forthcoming.

Only after I was successfully parked did I realise that there was no room to open any of the doors. Bugger. A bus conductor had leaned up against a lamp-post to watch my predicament as he ate a sandwich, and I smiled at him confidently. I would simply climb out of the boot. Inelegant, perhaps, but undoubtedly resourceful. I clambered over two sets of seats, cursing my decision to wear a skirt, and removed the parcel shelf so I could squeeze into the boot.

Did you know you can't open the boot of a car from the inside? I didn't. I mean, it makes sense, if you think about it: TV kidnappings would be much less dramatic if the victim, having been bundled unceremoniously into a car boot, could simply let themselves out. But really, who knew? With a heavy sigh I climbed back over two sets of car seats and reinstated myself in the driver's seat. Stubbornly refusing to meet the eye of the bus conductor, who was by now doubled up with mirth, I pulled forward a few feet, got out of the car, opened the boot, got back in the car, and reversed back into the space. I was starting to get a little hot and bothered by this point.

Getting by now really quite speedy at negotiating the two sets of car seats, I was soon in the back of the car, clambering out onto the pavement and slamming the boot triumphantly. I looked for my keys to lock the car. They were, of course, still in the ignition. Back into the boot I went. Back over two sets of car seats and into the driver's seat to get the keys, like a contestant in some sort of cross between *Top Gear* and *It's a Knockout*. The bus conductor had by this point been joined by two colleagues, and the three of them were almost apoplectic with laughter. I wouldn't let them get to me. All around me, frustrated drivers were leaving the car park, unable to find a space. But I had found one. Against all the odds, I had successfully parked my oversized car in a miniature space and lived to tell the tale.

Laugh all you like, I thought to myself as I locked the car and sailed nonchalantly towards the bus stop. I had won. The conductors grinned at each other as I approached, and I affected an air of polite indifference. One of them stepped forward.

'Excuse me, love,' he said. 'That space is for motorbikes: I'm afraid you're going to have to move your car.'

A mother's love

This morning I bent down at the school gate to give Josh a kiss, only for him to duck away. Suddenly too old for public displays of affection, he took his blushes into the classroom, where I couldn't embarrass him further.

A year younger than him, Evie and George are still free with their kisses, and their brother's reluctance makes me hold them a little tighter at the classroom door, newly conscious of the clock that ticks away such maternal closeness. Will it be next year they push me away? Or sooner, as they subconsciously take a lead from their sibling? I thought I might have a little longer, but I had forgotten the power of those good-natured jibes from friends, and the strength of the desire to be older than one's years.

At home, in private, the children remain deeply affectionate. They sprawl against me on the sofa, and fling their arms around me when night falls. They crawl into my bed when their worries grow too big, nestling into me as easily as if they were still part of me. They seek out warmth at every opportunity. Kisses – both offered and accepted – are numerous and indiscriminate; on the lips, on cheeks, on foreheads, tummies and necks. Sometimes soft, sometimes absent-minded, sometimes rushed.

Sometimes hard and unyielding; kisses that say *I love you,*
but by God I'm cross with you right now. In our house kisses
are the currency of love – never rationed, never condi-
tional, never refused.

'When will you be too big for us to do this?' I ask
George as we lie in near-darkness on the bottom bunk,
our arms entwined.

'Never!' comes the response, with a tight squeeze. 'I'll
still want to do this when I'm a hundred!'

But my breath catches, because I know that one day I
will lie with my children for the last time. I won't realise
it then, of course. I'll kiss them goodnight and go downstairs; load the dishwasher and put on the TV. And I'll
never lie down with them again. They might be ten when
it stops, or twelve, or fourteen, or eighteen, but there will
be a last time.

All these things we do without thinking: carrying our
children down the stairs, holding their hands as they cross
the road, cutting up their food when they're struggling
to use a knife. So fleeting, such a small part of our lives,
yet more important than anything else.

This is what our children will remember.

I can still recall the feeling of my mother's oilcloth
apron against my cheek as she pulled me towards her for
a cuddle. How old must I have been, I wonder, for my
head to be at waist height? Seven years old? Eight? I am
beyond there now, I realise, with the tops of three heads
already above waist height, a breath away from teenage
growth spurts and lanky limbs, from the surly grunts and
pendulum moods of adolescent angst.

I am there now, and I mustn't waste a moment.

Already I hoard obsessively the notes left by my bed, or on my desk for me to find once they've left for school. From *You're the best Mummy in the world!* and *I love you so much xx*, to *I'm sorry I was norty and maid you showt*, I keep them all. I stash them away in my bedside cupboard, in a folder grown fat with Post-its and scraps of paper, some bearing little more than a scribble, a heart, an *I love you.*

As for the school gate, I will gracefully accept defeat. I'll settle for a casual hair-ruffle instead of a lip-smacking goodbye; a nonchalant arm around a shoulder instead of an eager bear hug. I'll save my embarrassing kisses for home, when my oh-so-cool lad is just a little boy again, happy to curl up on the sofa with his mum. Whether he knows it or not, he needs cuddles for a few more years yet.

And, more importantly, so do I.

Time for bed

My best friend's husband had a vasectomy last week. It's become quite popular within my circle of acquaintances, which makes me realise I must now be middle-aged. It used to be tattoos and piercings – now it's all tummy tucks and sterilisation. A vasectomy seems to be quite the in thing among responsible men nowadays. I did wonder about getting my husband one for his birthday but the gift-card rack in WH Smith was sadly lacking, which is clearly an oversight. It would make a far more thoughtful present than Ferrari-driving or a hot-air balloon ride, and you could follow it up with a hernia op voucher for Christmas.

My friend Kate (she whose husband went under the knife) confided that she would not immediately be emptying the loft of the ten-year-old baby paraphernalia hidden within it. The doctor had explained it would take approximately thirty-six ejaculations before the procedure could be confirmed a success, and suggested they come back in four months for a test.

'Four months?' Kate exclaimed (having done some fast mental arithmetic). 'Should we not pencil something in for next year instead?' Her husband, barely able to conceal

his delight, patted her on the hand and nobly informed
the doctor they would do their utmost to comply. While
poor Kate viewed the prospect of thrice-weekly shenanigans as frankly exhausting, her mate bounded out of the
doctor's office like a lab off the leash, anxious to get
started.

This well-documented disparity between men and
women has absolutely nothing to do with sexual appetite
and everything to do with time. Women are simply too
busy. If you were to search my diary for a slice of time
in which to engage in rampant bedroom action (and I
wouldn't recommend it – it's desperately dull reading),
you won't find a single gap.

Assuming I sleep for eight hours each night (this is
hugely optimistic, given the yo-yo-like characteristics of
my children, but I live in hope), I am left with sixteen
hours in which to find time for a bit of marital hokey-
cokey. You might think that's quite a lot, but take out of
that the eight hours we are compelled to go to work (and
I'm told they take a dim view of sexual activity in the
workplace, should I be minded to pay my husband a visit)
and it leaves me with just eight. Just eight hours for a bit
of how's your father, while leaving time for life's other
demands. It's not a lot really, when you think about it.
And of course there are the children to manage. Left to
their own devices they have a tendency to self-destruct
and besides, I do rather like to play with the children
from time to time. It makes me feel like a real parent. So
that's another four hours spent supervising our offspring,
when I suppose I could be tying my husband to the

bedposts and licking whipped cream from his navel. Although frankly that's not going to help with the diet.

Food! Yet another demand on my time. By the time I've cooked a meal, dished up, eaten it and cleared it away, we can easily deduct another ninety minutes.

I'm down to two and a half hours, and that's before I've spent thirty minutes cleaning out the chickens and checking each one over for mysterious poultry diseases (not a task generally recommended to get you in the mood for romance, in case you were wondering. At least, it doesn't do it for me – I can't vouch for the chickens).

Of course my mother will ring, so that's at least another half an hour half listening to tales from the village, while tidying the playroom and kicking toy cars out from under the sofa. That reminds me – I've forgotten my husband's daily commute. That's a forty-minute journey each way, assuming he doesn't get stuck behind a tractor.

I think that's everything. Right, let's work this out . . . Eight hours at work, same again asleep, four being a parent, one and a half eating, half an hour on the chickens, same again on the phone and an hour and twenty when Rob's in the car. That leaves me with precisely ten minutes to get to heaven and back.

Oh, it's hardly worth it, is it?

MARCH

Springtime is the land awakening. The March winds are the morning yawn.

Lewis Grizzard

It is sometimes hard to believe that March means spring, when snow can turn St Patrick's Day white instead of green, and the winds are still fierce enough to take a trampoline three doors down. But spring it is – a wakening so gradual you hardly notice it.

If you look carefully at the drystone walls that border the fields you'll find nests of grass and wool hidden in the crevices, with clutches of speckled robin's eggs within. Ferns stretch their fronds outwards, their feet content in the damp darkness at the foot of the wall.

Here and there, the wall has collapsed. Honeyed stones form a chaotic cairn, waiting for the patience of the drystone-waller to pick up each one, to sort the sizes into piles and to bring new stone to replace what cannot be re-used. It is a job that won't be rushed, a job that has been carried out for centuries and will continue for centuries still. When it is finished, you will not see where the old and new meet, and soon the moss will grow again across this section of wall, for Mr and Mrs Robin to pluck for their nest.

You will see your first lamb of the year this month, impossibly small and clean against its mother's fleece, finding its feet in a field still filled with ponderous ewes. The next day you'll see another, then another, and suddenly there will be lambs everywhere, long-tailed and springing this way and that until it makes you dizzy to watch.

At home, you'll talk about how it won't be long before the grass will need cutting, and you'll risk putting clothes on the line, only to run out an hour later, pegs pinging across the garden as you snatch them out of the rain and into your basket. You'll put the kettle on, and grumble that it's really quite cold still, and isn't it supposed to be spring now?

On your walk, as you climb the stile to stroll a while along the winding road where few cars pass, there is a rustling up ahead, and a sudden jump, and there, by the hedge, as startled as you are, is a hare. So much bigger than a rabbit, so much bolder. He moves again, crossing the road as though he'd been waiting for the green man, before disappearing into the fields. If you'd been ten seconds earlier, ten seconds later, you'd have missed him.

Spring is easily missed in March, but if you watch from your window, if you take your tea into the garden and stand very still, you will see it. Spring is here.

Motherhood

There's a lot they don't tell you about having children. The fact that you'll never go to the loo on your own again, for example, or that when the kids leave home you'll still look just a tiny bit pregnant. They don't tell you how hard it is to get wax crayon off a skirting board, or how long it can take to potty-train.

And they don't tell you just how much you will love your children. That what you once thought was love – for your family, a boyfriend, even your husband – will pale into insignificance against the heart-clenching, all-consuming love you will feel for your children.

You're supposed to feel it instantly, the moment that mewling scrap of baby is placed on your breast, but that's something else they don't tell you: sometimes it doesn't happen.

I was still reeling from my first pregnancy when I fell for my second. Still spinning from four months in hospital visiting first two Perspex cribs, then just one. I spent nine months with a baby and a bump, totally unable to comprehend that a second set of twins would be arriving a little over a year after the first.

When they were born, I waited for the rush of love,

for the heady whirl of new motherhood, with its ups and downs, and tears and laughs. But it didn't come. Instead I felt a blanket of numbness descend over me, muting my senses and weighing me down so heavily I could barely drag myself through each day. I fed the babies, played with them, held them: all the time with an objectivity that made me feel I was watching the scene from afar, holding up marks out of ten. Had I been capable of reason, I would have been able to find explanations to ease my conscience. I was terrified of losing another child; too scared of doing something wrong; too broken by the events of the previous year.

I saw none of this. Felt nothing.

I knew there was something badly wrong, but piecing it together was like stirring treacle, and I couldn't see through the thick fog that seemed to envelop me from morning till night.

When help did come, it came swiftly.

The fog lifted, and suddenly I was living again. I still didn't feel the way a mother should, but I was taking tiny steps towards it. The twins were five months old when I felt the invisible cords of motherhood pulling me upstairs and into the darkened nursery, where I sat on the floor between the two cots. I listened to my sleeping babies breathing in turn, their soft sounds filling the room with tranquillity.

And then I felt it: a mother's love.

A tidal wave of warmth, which broke down all remaining defences and left smooth shores in its wake. My children breathed life back into my soul that night, and what I suddenly felt for them overwhelmed me. It was all I could do to stop myself from snatching them from their dreams and hugging them tight to my chest.

As the babies grew into toddlers, so I grew into a mother again. I found my way through the darkness of our beginning together, and poured months of emotion into each embrace.

Once love arrives, it never leaves. No matter what challenges motherhood throws at us, love lies just beneath the surface: underneath the arguments about untidy rooms and unfinished meals, beneath the chivvying to put on shoes and get to school. It sits quietly, politely, with no whoops or shouts to advertise its presence. It is all-encompassing, all-pervading, all-embracing, and the answer to everything.

There is nothing as pure, as strong or as welcome as the love of a mother for her child; and whether it arrives instantly or takes the scenic route, it stays for ever.

A room with a poo

Our house is on the market. Reluctantly we have agreed that with the growth of our brood, and the addition of more animals, we have finally outgrown our space.

We seem to be incapable of moving house the standard way; of making a measured decision to move, putting our own property up for sale, scouting around for a new one . . . Instead, as ever, we are going about things all wrong. An accidental discovery of a perfect house, swiftly followed by a mad scramble to paint skirting boards, weed the vegetable patch, and commit vast amounts of cash to an estate agent.

As I write, the house has been on the market for two weeks. It has never been so tidy, nor so clean. In fact, I suspect that, had Rob known I was capable of maintaining such high standards of domesticity, he would have suggested selling up years ago. The children have gamely accepted the removal of soft toys and posters of Manchester City players from their bedrooms, and dutifully make their beds each morning in case of 'aviewings'. My office, usually buried beneath piles of books, is minimalist and tranquil, my white-board wiped clean to avoid terrifying prospective buyers with notes on torture methods destined for a future novel.

The house may be in a permanent state of cleanliness, but there are still five people and a springer spaniel living here, making the pre-viewing Anneka Rice-style dash from room to room a necessity. I was addicted to programmes like *House Doctor* long before I had my own home, so I secretly love this element of selling a house. On the landing (to be removed to the car during viewings) lives a large plastic box: my very own house doctoring first aid kit. Out come the brand-new fluffy towels, the Jo Malone room fragrance and the ironed pillow cases. In go the toothbrush mugs, the bath mats with their damp footprints, and the pair of pants that has mysteriously appeared on George's bedside table. Duvets smoothed, blinds opened, doors closed, and a quick once-over with the vacuum cleaner. It's a doddle.

Viewings during school hours are, of course, a million times easier than those after 3 p.m., when the house is filled with PE kits, toast crumbs and homework. The children's enthusiasm for the house move stems largely from my habit of evacuating the entire family to the pub during viewings, where we order lemonades (them) and lager shandies (me) and try to crack fractions with the not-very-helpful interjections of the slightly worse-for-wear gentleman standing at the bar.

Our most recent viewing was on Saturday morning, when we mixed things up a little by going to a café for brunch.

'Does anyone need the loo?' I asked when we arrived. 'It's just through there.'

'S'okay,' the smallest one said. 'I did a ginormous poo just before we left.'

My heart sank. 'Which loo?' I demanded. 'How long before we left?'

'Upstairs,' smallest said. 'When we were getting our shoes on ready to leave.'

Shit, I thought. 'Please tell me you flushed.'

There was a long and loaded silence. I slumped in my chair. I knew without asking that said child would have left the bathroom door wide open, the loo seat up, the offending poo as big as a baby's arm proudly displayed in the pan. I imagined the prospective buyers exploring the downstairs rooms, delighting in the extended kitchen, the sunny sitting room, the scent of Jo Malone's lime, basil and mandarin fragrance in the air. And then, as they walk upstairs . . .

What's this? This heinous smell, assaulting my nostrils and making my eyes water? What ungodly presence lives in this house, that could create such a monstrous stench?

I wondered if I could somehow intercept them; phone the agent, race back to the house, prostrate myself upon the landing and refuse them access to upstairs until I could lock myself in the bathroom and flush the poo into submission.

My mobile rang. It was too late.

'All clear,' the estate agent said. 'You can come back now.'

How bad is the smell?

I was desperate to know, but too English to ask; the agent too English to tell me.

'I'm afraid they won't be making an offer,' he said apologetically.

'No,' I said with a sigh, 'I didn't think they would.'

Use them or lose them

I read a lot. Two or three books a week, often with several on the go at once. I read hardbacks, paperbacks, e-books. I read newspapers, magazines, blogs and columns, and if there's nothing else to read, I'll read the back of the cereal packet. An estate agent's sign. The label on the bottom of your shoe. I would no sooner leave the house without a book in my bag than I would walk down the high street in my pyjamas. I might have to stand in a queue for longer than a few seconds, and what would I do then?

I keep books in every room of the house. They are stashed in the glove boxes of both cars, along with the travel sickness bands, the portable oil-spill kit and the high-vis jacket, ready to be broken out at the first sign of emergency. Should I ever find myself stuck on the M5 for hours on end, I'll be ready. Bottles of water? Food rations? Pah! My priorities lie between the pages of a ripping yarn.

But right now, that's a bit of a problem. I pick up a novel, only to discard it twenty pages in. I peruse the shelves, scan countless blurbs, but nothing grabs me. The covers don't sing, the contents don't resonate. I have reader's block.

I read a vast number of crime and psychological thriller novels, and like anything consumed to excess, there is a fine line between enthusiasm and nausea. In my case, it's also hard to read a thriller without the voice in my head reminding me that what I'm reading isn't just a book: it's competition. Sometimes that voice is quiet. Sometimes it laughs out loud, taunting me with this oh-so-clever plot that *Don't you wish you'd thought of first?* And sometimes (and I won't pretend I'm proud of this) it's just the tiniest bit smug. *Nothing to worry about here . . .*

Perhaps, then, I wondered, my inability to read was not in fact reader's block, but a sudden aversion to *work* (let's face it, I wouldn't be the only one). I needed to switch things up a bit, but like a strict vegetarian suddenly fancying bacon, there wasn't a lot in the house. A few old Jilly Coopers, and a set of Maeve Binchys, but otherwise my fiction shelves were filled with blood, bodies and betrayal. I wasn't even sure what I was looking for, only that I wanted something completely different. I wondered if there was a dating app for stuck-in-a-rut readers, like bored housewives swiping right on Tinder, or a GP surgery where book doctors can write out prescriptions.

'Feeling under the weather? Try *The Music Shop* by Rachel Joyce.'

'Overdosed on Brexit news? Ah, Helene Hanff's *84, Charing Cross Road* will sort that out in a jiffy.'

Online shopping is all well and good, but Amazon's algorithms couldn't care less if you enjoy the Roy Orbison biography they suggested for you because you once accidentally clicked on the album when you were searching for your mum's Christmas present. They just want you to buy it.

No, there's only one place to cure reader's block, to push yourself out of your literary comfort zone, and to try something new without it costing you.

The library.

In the last decade, hundreds of public libraries have been closed down, with still more under threat. Aside from the community benefits offered by libraries – the warmth, the company, the internet, the education services – we are losing the expertise of thousands of librarians. Librarians who can listen to what you've enjoyed lately, and suggest something just as good you haven't yet tried. Librarians who can give you a jump start when you've stalled, with a graphic novel or a quirky memoir, or a *Have you tried anything by Linwood Barclay?* Librarians who know their way around their myriad bookshelves, and can put their finger on precisely what they – and you – need.

I went into my local library with nothing more concrete than 'no crime' in mind. I left with *Gin: A Global History*, Rick Stein's autobiography, *Eleanor Oliphant is Completely Fine* and *To Kill a Mockingbird*, which I hadn't read since school. With four such different books to dip into, and no pressure to enjoy (or even to read), I found I loved them all.

Reading block: cured.

If you haven't visited a library since you were a child, make this the month you do. Use them, or – as the saying goes – we'll lose them.

Extracting the pee

If ever I write a parenting manual it will include practical tips on things that really matter. Like how to wrestle a toddler into a car seat when their legs are splayed out like a starfish, or how to extricate yourself from the bed of a sleeping child without disturbing them.

I would dedicate an entire chapter to the tooth fairy. To a six-year-old there is little more exciting than the discovery of a wobbly tooth. From the second a hint of movement is detected, to the eventual extraction, the owner of said tooth thinks about little else. Every day is dedicated to the analysis, discussion and management of the wobbler, and the issue of cold hard cash plays a large part in conversations.

'The tooth fairy brings a golden coin for every tooth!' I remember Josh saying, long before his own teeth were ready to depart.

'Does she?' I said, horrified by the rate of inflation that had apparently occurred in Tooth Land since the 1980s. 'I thought she brought silver ones. Silver is *much* better.'

His eyes lit up. 'Silver coins – wow!'

Currency agreed, we settled on fifty pence, conceding that the first tooth would probably merit the full pound.

Imagine my horror when the childr
from school one day, before any wobb
to tell me that Rupert Accrington's too
and the tooth fairy had brought him fiv

FIVE POUNDS? That was a hundre   per
mouth! I could barely speak, I was so apoplectic with
rage. Raising the bar by giving children more than a
pound per tooth is completely unacceptable: a breach of
the Parental Code second only to buying bespoke jewel-
lery as an end-of-term teacher gift, when the rest of us
are wondering if we can get away with home-made fudge.
It simply shouldn't be done.

'Why does the tooth fairy give Rupert five pounds,
and only brings us fifty pee?' Evie asked.

'I imagine Rupert's mummy and daddy are rather well
off,' I said through gritted teeth. Too late, I realised my
mistake.

'But,' began Josh, always far too quick off the mark,
'why would it make any difference how much money
they have? It doesn't come from them.' As the cogs began
to whirr in his six-year-old head, I saw his childhood
innocence disappearing. Next step: Father Christmas. I
hastened to correct my error.

'No, of course it doesn't, darling, but tooth fairy money
is . . . er . . . sort of means tested. In reverse. She brings
more money to people who already have it, because
they're . . . er . . . used to it. And we're not.' As arguments
went, it was somewhat flawed.

'Well, that seems like a rubbish way of giving out
money. It should go to the people who need it, and

ss out the rich people altogether.' Politicians, take note.

As we enter the pre-teen years, those few milk teeth remaining are already loose, and this particular source of income will soon draw to a close. When the children aren't talking about how much filthy lucre they will garner for their teeth, they're discussing how to hasten the extraction. Like women exchanging diet tips at the gym, they swap anecdotes over their after-school snacks.

'Anna's came out when she ate an apple. Can I have an apple, Mummy?'

'If you twist it when you wobble it, the root breaks more easily.'

On and on and on.

When Evie triumphantly showed me her latest wobbly tooth, I fully expected it to come out that evening. But on it clung, despite heroic efforts from its owner, and weeks later it was still hanging on by a thread, the replacement tooth already coming through behind it.

'You could just give it a yank,' I said, half repelled, half fascinated.

She shook her head. 'I can't.' I didn't blame her.

'I'll do it,' said Josh cheerfully, himself an old hand at losing teeth. Evie opened her mouth wide and didn't bat an eyelid as Josh reached in and gave a sharp tug.

'It's out!' she cried gleefully, unperturbed by the blood pouring from her mouth. 'Now the tooth fairy will come!'

So excited by the prospect of fifty pence was she, I half expected her to ask Josh to tackle a few more gnashers.

'Well done, Josh,' I said, rather proud of such gallantry. 'I think I'll be a dentist when I'm older,' he said.

An excellent career choice. Perhaps then he can pay me back for all these teeth.

Swimming against the tide

I am making a concerted effort to regain my pre-baby figure. Well, actually I'm aiming for someone else's figure – mine has never really been up to much. I've taken to visiting the gym before work but since January, when presumably everyone began their new fitness regimes, it has got terribly busy. Last Wednesday I took one look at the gym, with its heaving mass of sweating bodies, and decided to give it a miss. The pool was deliciously empty, and although I hadn't checked in at reception I had my swimming costume in my gym bag. I made a snap decision to go for a swim instead. I'm not a great swimmer, and I find the whole concept of lane swimming a bit alarming. How does one know which lane to choose? I'm definitely faster than the old ladies straining to keep their hair dry, but I'm not quite ready for the fast lane – in many respects. I worry about picking a seemingly empty lane, only to be confronted with a rubber head emerging from nowhere with an enormous gasp of breath.

I can't abide the unisex changing areas you find in leisure centres nowadays. They call ours a changing village, which is a bit optimistic considering it doesn't have any of the amenities one might expect from a village, like a problem with dog poo or a post office fighting closure. It's all a bit open plan for my liking. It feels uncomfortably voyeuristic watching someone soaping their armpits, and I always seem to bump into someone I know. I once showered with Mr Eldridge from the town council, a total gentleman who maintained firm eye contact throughout. Suffice to say Councillor Manning wasn't so discreet.

I would far prefer different changing areas for men and women. In fact, they should consider having a separate section altogether for women who have had children. It would save the embarrassment, half an hour after swimming, when a gallon of pool water inexplicably and uncontrollably escapes from between your legs as though you've been smuggling a water balloon.

On this occasion I negotiated the changing village and dutifully queued up for my pre-swim shower. The showers cause a bit of a bottleneck and there was a line of at least half a dozen people in front of me. I hopped around trying to avoid clumps of hair while I waited for my turn. The woman in front turned and smiled. 'First time?'

'No,' I said, 'I have been before. Not for a while, though.'

'Oh, you'll love it.' She smiled. 'It's really friendly.'

How odd, I thought. Still, nice of her to chat. I realised with mild curiosity that everyone in the queue was wearing sleek black costumes and matching swimming hats complete with goggles. Clearly the morning swim session was a serious one. I felt somewhat out of place in my floral monstrosity. The gigantic pink flowers do nothing for my bottom, but the steel-girder stomach panel stops me scaring small children.

The queue moved forward and I suddenly caught sight of a large sign propped on a chair by the large glass window looking on to reception.

Closed to the public – Swim Club.

Bugger. That explained the swimming hats.

By now several people had joined the queue behind me, and we were shuffling out of the shower area and lining up next to the pool. I had a quick mental run-through of my options. Perhaps I could brazen it out. I mean, it's not like I can't swim at all. How hard could it be?

The first swimmer cut cleanly through the surface and shot away like a bullet. My chances of passing unnoticed when I flopped off the side like a pregnant walrus were looking rather slim. This called for desperate measures. I clutched my calf and let out a pained cry. The woman in front turned again.

'Cramp?'

I nodded bravely.

'Oh, you poor thing – you'd better sit this one out till it passes.'

I hobbled to the back of the queue and retreated into the changing village, where I pulled on my clothes over my swimsuit and scuttled out through reception. I mentally deleted swimming from my fitness action plan and went for a latte instead. I must have burned off a couple of hundred calories running from the pool, so I had a muffin as well. And a pain au chocolat. Exercise makes me awfully hungry.

No easy answers

I have never lied to my children about the big things in life: birth, death, the birds and the bees. As a result, they are terrifyingly matter-of-fact about them. A favourite game when they were younger involved one child lying underneath a rug in the playroom, while the other two knelt solemnly on either side.

'What are you playing?' an unwitting visitor once asked them.

'Graveyards,' came the cheery response. 'Get out now, George, it's my turn in the coffin.'

I've always worked on the basis that if they're old enough to ask about something they're old enough to know, and so when Josh asked how babies got out of their mummies' tummies (a far easier question to answer than how they got in there) I told him. His eyes widened, and he giggled a bit, but he seemed to take it on the chin and didn't have nightmares that night. I mentioned that it might be wise not to talk about it with the other three- and four-year-olds at pre-school, whose parents might not yet have told them the gory details of childbirth, and he promised he wouldn't.

Josh was true to his word, although I should have

perhaps included adults in my warning, because it was in the supermarket a few weeks later that he decided to impart his knowledge.

'I came out of Mummy's vagina,' he said to the checkout girl conversationally. She blanched a little. Everything suddenly went rather quiet. The man in the queue behind us coughed.

Clearly not content with the reaction of his audience, Josh decided to add a little more detail to the picture. 'It stretched THIS BIG!' he said, holding out his arms as wide as he could. I grew rather hot and pretended to be fascinated by the contents of my purse.

Perhaps Josh picked up on my distress. Perhaps he is a natural gentleman. Perhaps he caught the alarmed expression of the man behind us, who wasn't quite sure where to put his courgette. I don't know. Whatever the reason, he clearly felt it necessary to redress the balance and defend my honour, because he leaned forward to his now-enraptured audience.

'Don't worry,' he stage-whispered, 'it stretched back.'

Controversially among my peers, we have always opted for accurate gynaecological terms in our house. A penis is a penis, after all, not a todger, a winkie or a John Thomas. And a vagina is a vagina, not a twinkle, a Mary or a front bottom. While I confess to flirting with some alternatives to penis (I find willies fairly acceptable) I have failed to identify a female version that doesn't make me cringe. I'm not sitting in a doctor's surgery discussing frou-frous and minkys, and surely keeping tuppence in your pants is just asking for trouble. I didn't want to ruin bedtime stories by labelling them fairies, and there was a whole range of words to which I wouldn't even give house room: I don't mean to be a snob, but no daughter of mine was ever going to have a fanny . . .

Last week one of the children (I shall preserve their anonymity on this occasion, for reasons which will become clear) returned from school a little downcast, having been told off for using the word penis.

'We have to say *privates* instead,' the others said, confirming a school rule which appeared to ban the use of body-part terminology.

'How ridiculous!' I exploded. 'There is absolutely nothing rude about the correct use of an anatomical term, and to consider it so is symptomatic of a sexually repressed nation. I will not have my children criticised simply for being articulate and mature.' I finally took a breath and began composing a letter of complaint in my head. 'Why were you talking about penises, anyway?' I said, wanting to get my facts straight before I started writing. 'What was it you said?'

There was a long pause and an exchange of looks, and I felt a familiar sense of misgiving.

'"You penis head",' came the response.

'Ah,' I said, mentally screwing up my letter. 'Yes, that is rather rude.'

Hostess with the mostes'

'Take my mother-in-law,' the old joke goes. 'No, really, please take her.'

Well, please don't. Out of all the mothers-in-law I could have ended up with, I hit pay dirt with mine, who is not only glamorous, fun and great company, but has yet to give me oven gloves or anti-wrinkle cream for Christmas. In fact she specialises in those sorts of gifts you desperately wanted to buy for yourself, but simply couldn't justify doing so. Nor does she confine herself to special occasions; if you go and stay the night at her lovely Burford home, you are very likely to find a small gift waiting on your dinner plate. Entertaining is my mother-in-law's forte. Her house is filled with beautiful things, the kitchen packed with M&S nibbles and the wine rack never empty. Even a simple mid-week stopover is like checking into the most luxurious boutique guest-house, with piles of fluffy towels in the bathroom, and baskets of miniature toiletries, sparkling water and carefully chosen magazines in the bedroom. This is so unlike my own home, where overnight guests are greeted by child-related chaos, a pull-out bed in my office, and an unholy smell coming from the downstairs loo, that I sink into her house like a marathon runner into a warm bath. It is utter bliss.

Soon after Evie and George were born, my mother-in-law had her loft converted into two bedrooms so the grandchildren could stay more often (told you she was good). The larger room was for the twins, complete with two single beds. When grown-up couples came to stay, the beds cleverly converted to a double bed made up in soothing cream linens and soft fur throws.

Soon after the room had been finished, I was enjoying a quiet coffee with my mother-in-law at Burford Garden Centre when she announced that she would have to get back to get the room ready for her friend Alice, who was staying the night.

'I'll have to make up the double,' she said, 'and it's quite tricky to pull it together.'

Could Alice not sleep in a single bed, I wondered?

'Well, no,' replied my mother-in-law, looking furtively about as though Alice might suddenly appear at another table, 'she's rather – well, you know, rather *large*.'

It transpired that my mother-in-law had a strict system in place: guests boasting an acceptable dress size were allocated a single bed, while any unfortunates likely to frequent plus-size stores were tactfully prepared a larger one, presumably in case they fell out.

I couldn't help but feel this was a risky strategy – what would happen if my mother-in-law were reunited with an old friend, inviting her to stay only to discover she had piled on the pounds in the intervening years? Would she discreetly withdraw in order to alter the sleeping arrangements? I began to feel my pull-out office bed was perhaps rather simpler and less stressful. Perhaps I could start to dress up the experience a little – a bottle of water and some magazines should be achievable, even for me. A quick root around the sitting room revealed two copies of the *Postal Advertiser* and the cover of a Spider-Man comic. I just don't seem to have the hospitality gene.

Fortunately I am far more often a guest in someone else's home than I am the hostess in my own, and I leapt at the opportunity last week to stay at my mother-in-law's for the night, following a 'bit of a do' near by. It was hard to decide what I was looking forward to the most: my G&T-accompanied bath before going out, the cup of tea and precautionary paracetamol waiting for me on my return, or the breakfast in bed brought to me in the morning. Arriving in Burford as early as I dared, I followed my mother-in-law up the stairs to the guest room, my overnight bag bumping against my legs.

Stepping back slightly on the landing to allow me into the room, she said breezily, 'I made up the double for you – I thought you'd be more comfortable that way,' and turned to go, to leave me to unpack. Ever the hostess, she paused on the top step. 'Can I get you something to eat before you go out? Some sausage rolls perhaps, or a sand-wich?'

I contemplated the sleeping arrangements.

'No thanks,' I told her. 'I think I'd better pass.'

Home is where the art is

I am surely not the only mother who always dreaded the sight of my children clutching armfuls of drawings and junk models as they poured out of school. 'Look, Mummy!' they would cry when we eventually got home. They'd brandish badly drawn pictures in my face, scarcely able to stand still, such was their excitement at this latest artistic endeavour.

'That's lovely, darling,' I'd say. 'Now pop it in the recycling box, and go and get ready for swimming.'

You can't keep everything, can you? Our recycling is mercifully free from paintings nowadays, but at their creative peak my three children produced at least a dozen 'works of art' each week (not to mention the castles built from loo roll and painted with Farrow & Ball tester pots) – just where was it supposed to go?

I liked my house. I liked the sage green walls in the kitchen and the tastefully arranged Emma Bridgewater pottery. I liked my arty photographs, my scatter cushions and the sculpture we got as a wedding present from Sophie and Ian. I never felt the house would be improved by badly crayoned pictures of me with no hair and teeth bigger than my hands, stuck up haphazardly with Blu Tack and pieces of peeling Sellotape. I didn't want models made of yoghurt pots, PVA glue dripping between the cracks, gracing my occasional tables.

And I don't do glitter. Anywhere.

Like every parent, I think my children are immensely talented, but Banksy they're not. If the kids have spent a lot of time on a drawing, or produced something truly lovely, I'll put it on the fridge for a while before it goes in the art file for posterity. But I don't plaster the walls with the children's art, and you won't find it in the sitting room – that's strictly a grown-up space.

At the end of one fateful term I was in school for my weekly 'parent helper' session. I used to love these afternoons: I helped with French, science, ICT . . . whatever the class was doing, and I revelled in two hours away from emails, phone calls and deadlines.

On the day in question the children were making calendars to take home for their parents. Painted handprints had been turned into animals and plants, the resulting page had been backed with card, and finally the children were painstakingly tying pieces of ribbon to the top and stapling diary pages to the bottom.

'It's an awful lot of work for something that'll end up in the bin, isn't it?' I said casually to the class teacher, who was fighting with the laminator. She stopped and looked at me, aghast.

'Why would they end up in the bin?'

This was a turn-up for the books: did teachers actually expect parents to keep things?

I faltered. 'Um, because that's what I do with mine.'

There was a loaded silence and I rushed to fill it. 'It all takes up room, doesn't it?' I said, desperately trying to justify my actions. 'And this sort of thing,' I held up a cock-eyed handprint embellished with yellow splodges on the end of each finger, 'I mean, what's it even supposed to be?'

'It's a bunch of daffodils,' the teacher said, with more than a trace of coolness. At that point I felt it wise to let the subject drop, and we worked in silence until the calendars were finished and handed back to their owners to take home, where I felt certain most were destined for the recycling box. The children sat on the carpet and I wished them all a happy half term.

'Just a moment,' the teacher said as I picked up my bag. 'We've got something for you, to say thank you for coming in every week.'

There was a flutter of excitement from the carpet and my heart began to melt. I didn't expect anything, of course I didn't, but how kind of them all to think of me. I wondered if it might be chocolates, or perhaps a bottle of wine.

The teacher handed me an envelope, a hint of amusement on her face, and I didn't need to open it to know what I would find inside.

'I do hope you like it,' she said. 'I believe they're meant to be daffodils.'

APRIL

April showers bring forth May flowers.

Proverb

Cow parsley explodes in every hedgerow, and you can put up with the showers because without it how could the Cotswolds possibly be so green? You had no idea there were so many different greens; that you could look down on the valleys and count twenty shades from chartreuse to jade, emerald to olive. The April rains are a small price to pay, and anyway, at least it isn't so *cold* any more.

There are flowers everywhere now. Narcissi, gathered at the base of trees and in self-made bunches throughout the churchyards; primroses giving colour to a shady corner of the garden. Clematis climbs upwards, silver-pink flowers seeking the sun, and the cherry tree bursts into blossom you pray won't be lost to the weather.

The hedgehogs are awake, and you put out a bowl for them, remembering to use cat food instead of the bread and milk you offered as a child. You cut out an article on making bee hotels from bamboo sticks, and never quite get round to it, but they seem to be happy enough in your garden nevertheless. You give in to an urge to spring clean the house – an urge that passes two hours later, when you have taken everything out of every cupboard in the kitchen, and now face the prospect of putting it back.

The changing clocks have given you an extra hour of daylight. You marvel at the way it is light as you cook supper, and then that it is still light as you finish eating. Soon it will be light enough to go for a walk before bed, and to feel the crispness in the air that arrives as soon as the warmth of the sun dies down.

You spy brown-blotched chaffinch eggs in nests shaped like perfect cups, lined with cosy down and wrapped in thick moss, and for a fortnight you go back each day, until a furious chirping as you approach tells you not to disturb. You go instead to Foxholes, where the woodland falls gently away towards the River Evenlode, and a narrow forest path meanders through a blanket of bluebells. It is breath-takingly beautiful, even though it is raining again, and really, haven't we had enough rain yet? Your umbrella catches on trees, and your boots splash in the puddles, and you exchange a cheery *Lovely spring we're having!* with the dog walkers you pass, who are equally cheery because even in the rain the bluebells are beautiful. The bluebells are everything.

Broken nights

They say youth is wasted on the young. You know what else they fritter away? Sleep. Like most of us, I spent much of my teenage years in bed, grunting when the alarm went off for school, and rolling my eyes at any event scheduled any earlier than midday. Even in my twenties my capacity to sleep was worthy of an Olympic gold medal; I thought nothing of curling up under a nightclub table and catching forty winks while my hardier friends partied away the hours.

Police shift work served only to strengthen the bond with my duvet. I would drive home from Oxford after a night shift, fall into bed at eight o'clock, then scramble to get up and dressed in time for that evening's shift, a full fourteen hours later. Neither light nor noise troubled me; I could literally sleep anywhere, any time. Like most enjoyable things in life (disposable income, perky breasts, a pelvic floor . . .) sleep disappeared once I had children. Well, strictly speaking, as soon as I fell pregnant, when my wails about thrice-nightly toilet trips were met with sage head-nodding from my parent peers.

'That's your body getting you ready for night feeds,' I was told.

Mother Nature's a bitch, I realised afterwards. Could she not have instead enabled us to bank several thousand hours of sleep – camel-like – to be released months later, when our babies are teething and colicky, and sleep is something that happens to other people? Apparently not. So sleep and I broke up in 2006, and have since then shared only fleeting moments together; the occasional one-night stand in a dark hotel room, and once – daringly – in the marital bed, when the children were away and I had no place else to be in the morning.

But for the most part sleep is a luxury I no longer enjoy. Years of listening out for babies means I wake at the slightest sound; the milk delivery, next door's dog, the foxes in the woods at the back of the house. While the children generally sleep straight through, they are young enough to need their mother should they have a bad dream, or when they wake with a worry that can't wait till morning. I am adept at clearing up vomit with my eyes shut, at yawning my way through a lullaby, and making up stories in the dead of night. Come morning, the offending child bounces happily to the breakfast table, while I drag myself downstairs like an extra from *The Walking Dead*, persuaded from my bed only by the lure of caffeine.

Even a night free from child disturbances is not an unbroken one. I have long accepted the permanence of the 3 a.m. wee – perfecting the art of navigating my way to the bathroom and back with my eyes shut – but I am less enthusiastic about the recent appearance of the 1 a.m. anxiety call. *Did you do the packed lunches?* it whispers, prodding me awake. *You know I did*, I respond. But it won't be silenced. *You know you've got a column deadline this week, don't you? And two birthday presents to buy. And the committee meeting on Tuesday's been moved to Wednesday, and there are avocados in the fridge that need eating.* On and on it whispers, till my head feels tight with pressure, and I am more awake than if someone had thrown cold water in my face.

I know all that! I tell my head. *It's all under control. The column is half-written, the presents are ordered, the meeting's in the diary and I'm making guacamole tomorrow.*

'You worry too much,' my husband said when I told him about the 1 a.m. anxiety call.

'I'm not worried about avocados,' I told him, worrying then that I came across as the sort of person who worries about avocados. I explained that the anxiety call doesn't present me with huge problems to solve at 1 a.m. The anxiety call specialises in insignificant, pointless details, presented to me with the sole purpose of waking me up and keeping me awake. I tried making a list before going to bed; the idea being that I could offload my problems in an organised way, reassuring my brain that everything was under control. *Make guacamole*, I wrote (having forgotten once again to do so). I woke at one as usual. *What if the avocados have gone off? You won't be able to make guacamole.* The voice was judgemental. *Then I'll throw them away*, I told it boldly. *What will you make instead? If you checked them now, you'd know if they were off, and you could make a plan.*

My head was beginning to seriously piss me off. *I'm not checking the avocados at one in the morning*, I told it firmly.

That's ridiculous. It carried on nagging me. *You know the food bin needs emptying, don't you? You've been meaning to do it for days. Why don't you do it now?*

I lay in bed, my eyes squeezed shut. I would not go downstairs. I would not empty the food bin. I would not check the bloody avocados. Slowly, I succeeded in muting the voice. I concentrated on my breathing. In and out, in and out. I lay in the dark, realising that not only was I wide awake, I now needed the loo. I sighed, and peeled myself from beneath the covers; padded to the bathroom and back again. I paused by the bedroom door. Now that I was up, I might as well check those avocados.

Business or pleasure?

Talk to anyone who travels regularly for business and they'll tell you the same thing: the novelty soon wears off.

'There's never time to see anything,' they complain, shuttled, as they are, between airport and hotel.

It's exhausting, they say. It's tedious. It's not remotely as glamorous as it sounds. They miss their home comforts, they miss their kids, they miss their spouse's home-cooked meals.

They're missing the point.

I admit I'm relatively new to the business traveller role – in twelve years as a police officer I rarely got further than Slough – but I can't see the novelty wearing off any time soon. Since my first book came out I've spent almost as many nights away as I have in my own bed, and each one still fills me with joy. So what if the hours spent on a train or plane outnumber those on stage by eight to one? That's eight hours' uninterrupted travelling time. Four hours on a train, each way, with a hot cup of tea and no one wanting to use the loo, sit on my lap or play Top Trumps (I'm referring to my children here; my husband is marginally less demanding). Four hours to crack on with my current work in progress, without the doorbell ringing, the phone going (*Sorry, can't talk, I'm in the quiet carriage*), or next door's dog going ballistic when I open the back door. I am more productive on a train than anywhere else, and love nothing more than the promise of an overnighter in a nice hotel.

My friend Tina is a professional jet-setter. She hates travelling so much that when she takes a week off work she spends it holed up in her flat, refusing even to drive to the shops.

'It's just one anonymous hotel room after another,' she sighs, when asked about her latest raft of trips.

But that, in my view, is precisely the point. Who doesn't love a hotel room? Air conditioning, heavy curtains, piles of pillows, and a bed so big you can starfish all night and never touch the sides. Kettle, shortbread, mini-bar . . . what more could you ask for? And that's before you've slipped on a fluffy bathrobe and raided the toiletries for miniature shampoos and shower caps (top tip: these make excellent salad bowl covers for alfresco eating back home).

Go on holiday somewhere exotic and you're duty bound to go out and explore, but when you're away on a work trip the pressure is off. You can legitimately spend whatever free time you have lolling on that enormous bed, watching Netflix and ordering tax-deductible nachos. Home-cooked meals? Who cares? If I'm not eating home-cooked food, it means I'm not cooking it either, and that's good enough for me. I appreciate a good meal, but if I were judging *MasterChef* I'd dish up fewer points for taste and presentation, and far more for the semi-finalist who writes a shopping list, battles their way round the supermarket with three children, unpacks the bags, realises they've forgotten the milk, goes out again, comes back, cooks supper AND washes up. Preferably while making the packed lunches and finding lost PE kits. When that's your culinary reality I can assure you that a slightly dry burger and a pile of greasy chips begin to assume Michelin-star properties.

As for the morning after . . . Is there anything better than a hotel breakfast? The delicious indecision: should you order room service, or pop downstairs with the paper and your room key, roaming the buffet like a lion circling gazelle? The extravagance of ordering brown *and* white toast, and the gastronomic confusion that comes from eating slices of cheese and salami this early in the morning. Charcuterie for breakfast! How terribly European. Rice Krispies and a Nescafé at your kitchen table are never going to compare.

As someone who – when at home – is abruptly dragged from slumber by arguments about who finished the orange juice and do-we-really-have-to-clean-our-teeth, the polite deference of a hotel I-do-hope-you-enjoyed-your-stay is sheer bliss.

In fact, there's only one thing lovelier than a trip away, and that's the welcome I get when I come home.

One not-so-careful driver

It's fair to say that driving isn't my strong point. Looking back, the signs were there early on, when I failed my test after hitting a slow-moving lorry as I turned out of the test centre.

'Would you like to carry on?' the examiner said.

'Is there any point?' I asked.

There wasn't.

I did eventually pass; a year later, when the time of my test coincided with a rush hour so congested I was taken out on the open roads, where there were no roundabouts, no traffic lights, no lanes.

I loved driving, back then. I remember that first solo trip, in my mother's Metro, laughing out loud with the windows down and Madonna's 'Vogue' on the cassette player. My parents were generous with the use of their cars, and with the petrol to fill them (no doubt relieved to no longer be ferrying my sisters and me to parties and pubs) and I didn't buy a car of my own until I went to university. I can't say I loved that Vauxhall Nova, but I loved what it allowed me to do.

Just before I graduated I wrote it off in crawling traffic on the M25, in a disappointingly undramatic bump which didn't leave a mark on the Range Rover in front of me but sent my fifteen-year-old Nova to the scrapyard. I needed a new car, and I knew exactly what I wanted. I'd had a boyfriend who drove a light blue MG Midget: the boyfriend hadn't lasted, but the Midget had lingered in my heart. I found one in the small ads, and drove it away feeling happier than I'd ever felt behind a wheel. Primrose yellow, chrome-bumpered, and almost a decade older than I was, she was everything I wanted in a car. I put the roof down whenever it wasn't raining (and sometimes when it was), and loved the waves from other MG drivers, and the tacit permission it gave for conversations with strangers.

I broke down a lot, but I didn't care.

I *did* care when I pulled out at a roundabout too late to avoid the car I had thought was turning off. The bump cracked their headlight; it wrote off my beloved Midget. Undeterred, I bought the car back as scrap and had it rebuilt. We were back on the road. Later, when a joint mortgage brought an end to selfish spending, my parents bought a half share in the Midget, slowing the rust by keeping it in their garage, and gradually paying for more and more of my share until I could hardly pretend it was mine.

We (they) had her resprayed British racing green, and had tan leather seats fitted. My dad and I took her to Le Mans, limping back on the ferry with a broken handbrake and an exhaust belching black fumes in our wake. She still lives in my parents' garage, and I harbour secret hopes of seeing my own children behind her wheel. In the meantime, I needed something more reliable. I bought a Smart car and managed not to write it off, but only because I swapped cars one day with my husband-to-be and wrote off his instead, overshooting a T-junction and landing in a ditch in a cloud of airbag smoke.

'It's just metal,' Rob shrugged, relieved I was unhurt, and stoical about the loss of his car.

Rather than getting better at driving, I seemed to be getting worse.

Attending a burglary in progress in a marked police car, I released my seatbelt on my approach, to facilitate a swift exit. I remember the shock of a humpback bridge I didn't know was there, and the feeling of space between tarmac and tyres, and then . . . nothing.

I was lucky. So very lucky.

The crash shook me up, and it also woke me up. I was finally driving carefully. As our family expanded, so did my cars. A Renault Scenic was replaced by a hideous orange Ford Galaxy, the only vehicle big enough to squeeze in three car seats and a triple buggy. My gleeful, Madonna-playing, open-road days belonged to someone else, and I secretly dreaded any journey longer than twenty minutes. The whingeing, the are-we-there-yets, the raisins and breadsticks and all-too-frequent vomiting . . .

For ten years, driving has been a chore, a punishment, a necessary evil. But as of today I am the proud owner of a cappuccino-coloured Fiat 500. There are no car seats, no muddy boots, no wellies or buggies or armfuls of shopping. No roof rack for bikes. Just me, in a dinky car with bags of personality, and cheery waves from other Fiat

500 fans. Madonna on the stereo, the window down, and the biggest smile on my face.

I've finally fallen in love with cars again – and this time, I'm driving carefully.

Facebook break-up

Apparently the most anxiety-inducing event of one's life is moving house; comparable only to death and divorce. Since our house stubbornly refuses to sell, I can't corroborate this from recent experience, but I'll tell you what *is* stressful: your spouse joining Facebook.

For years I've been happily waxing lyrical on social media, in the knowledge that my husband was blissfully unaware of my rants. *It seems teabags don't walk to the bin on their own*, I might – somewhat passive-aggressively – have posted. *Who knew?* Cue a series of empathetic likes and comments from friends married to teabag-abandoners and toothpaste-lid-leaver-offers. Hardly a scintillating conversation-starter, I'll accept, but the sort of water-cooler banter in which the work-at-home freelancer tends to engage on social media. Who else is there to hear our woes, but the postman and our 564-strong list of Facebook friends?

Don't get me wrong, I wasn't entirely without discretion. I'd never have posted about that frustrating habit Rob has of disappearing to the bathroom at the exact moment supper is ready, or detailed the fungal infection he had back in 2001, but run-of-the-mill gripes are fair game in social media land.

Being the sort of person who is liable to combust if required to keep exciting news to herself, Facebook was also my go-to platform for surprises. *Three days to go!* I disclosed to my (naturally enraptured) friends, beneath a photograph of the hotel I had booked as a birthday surprise.

Last week Rob went away for a week. As I worked I could hear the dulcet tones of the builder singing to himself as he installed a bathroom suite, ready for the ta-da moment on Friday evening. Pre husband-on-Facebook days, I might have documented the highs (*All on track, love – your hubby's going to be dead chuffed*) and lows (*You should probably take a look at these damp floorboards . . .*) of said installation, in my own online version of *DIY SOS*. But now? Now there's no point even taking photos. Posting general status updates has entirely lost its allure now that my audience is so close to home.

'Hey, I saw Jack and Sally today,' I'll say cheerily as my husband arrives back from work.

'Yes, you went to that new place in the high street, didn't you?' he'll say, pre-empting my next gambit. 'The carrot cake looked nice.'

I open my mouth to ask about his day, then remember I already know, thanks to the status update he posted an hour ago. At this rate we'll be able to give up talking altogether.

My friend Judy is convinced she has the answer. She and her husband both have Facebook accounts, with many mutual friends, but they are not themselves connected.

'I couldn't stand it,' she tells me. 'It was like having someone standing over my shoulder, watching me type.'

I know just how she feels.

Oops, I posted, just the other week. *Had to sign the late book at school . . . again.* Seconds later there were footsteps on the stairs. Rob's face appeared round my office door.

'If you made the packed lunches the night before,' he said helpfully, 'you'd give yourself an extra ten minutes in the morning.'

Wisely, he retreated before I could find something to throw at him.

I wondered if this responsiveness could work in my favour.

Deadline panic, I posted, the following day. *Tea needed!*

I waited. And waited.

Nothing.

Clearly spousal selective deafness also applies to Facebook. Should I unfriend him? It seems a little harsh. Perhaps we could have a trial social media separation. Message other people. It'll hurt at first, of course, but before too long there'll be a kitten gif to raise a smile; that video of Trump and the blow-away hair. We'll get through it. I wait until dinner to broach the subject, but the right opportunity doesn't come up. I try again before bed, and again at breakfast, but can't find the right words.

There's only one thing for it. I'll have to let him know via Facebook.

Lice to see you again

The children are scratching their heads. Either they're fretting over their times tables, or the nits are back.

Scourge of the primary-school parent, headlice very nearly prevented me having any children at all. I shuddered to hear of friends who were infested on a weekly basis with the little critters, and the thought of tackling them myself proved an effective psychological contraception for some time. But rather like the fear that you'll never be able to stomach a vomiting child, or wipe someone else's snotty nose, somehow once you finally have children Mother Nature takes over and replaces your queasiness with a large dose of parental stoicism.

I can't say that I relish the task of ferreting through my daughter's curls like a chimpanzee, but it isn't nearly as ghastly as I'd imagined. I do, however, feel faintly aggrieved by the loss of that childhood figure, the school nit nurse. I'm told her demise has less to do with financial cutbacks and more to do with the Equality and Human Rights Commission; apparently it's embarrassing and humiliating for children to line up for inspection. One teacher at my children's school told me she wasn't even allowed to tell the parents if she saw lice in their child's hair.

'All we can do is send a letter to every parent advising them we have an outbreak,' she said. Her hands were tied, she explained; some parents had complained about victimisation and now policy was quite clear. No one should be singled out. Horrified by the thought that, unbeknown to me, my children might be crawling with lice, I made her promise to circumvent protocol with a knowing look and a coded message, should she see so much as a single nit on my offspring's heads.

'The chemist has got some of that *special shampoo you like*,' she was to say, winking broadly in case I'm too dense to catch her drift.

Nowadays I'm a veteran in such matters, but this week's infestation adds another chore to an already packed day, making it now imperative that the children have a bath before bed tonight, despite it being only Wednesday, and an all-over wash not due for at least another four days.

Just as the nit nurse was part of the fabric of my schooldays, so the Sunday-night bath – with a swirling dollop of Matey – was a well-established ritual. Unless my sisters and I were unusually filthy, I don't recall being encouraged to bathe more frequently until long after I'd left behind the knee-high socks and pinafore of primary school. Yet now every parenting book prescribes a warm bath as an essential part of the evening routine, advocating gentle massage with carefully selected oils as a 'relaxing part of the mother and baby bonding process'.

Reading such books is like hearing about a mythical world. At no point in my parenting experience has bathtime ever been relaxing. Washing my three is like forcing a flock of wayward sheep through a chemical dip without the assistance of a trained collie.

The children love taking baths as much as I hate giving them and will chase each other up the stairs, shedding clothes like streakers at a rugby match. Once on the landing they starburst, revelling in a game of naked hide-and-seek in which I am the only loser. I run the bath and duck, as three successive splashes soak the bathroom floor. From there on in it's one long slippery game of catch, made bearable only by the fact that bathtime happily coincides with gin o'clock.

Such antics mean that washing is sporadic in our house and driven by necessity. I claim our aversion to baths is driven by a keen desire to reduce water consumption (we save a lot of water this way). But tonight there will be no avoiding it – it's time to don my rubber gloves and go on nit patrol. I may be some time.

The body shop

I've stopped reading the glossies. Well, except *Cotswold Life*, of course. The problem is that they are full of glamorous women with stomachs so taut you could bounce Maltesers off them; the only full-bodied thing about them is their hair, swishing across tanned shoulders. It's terribly depressing. Rob doesn't understand my aversion to such impossibly beautiful women. He likens it to his avid reading of the property sections in lifestyle magazines: 'I'll never be able to afford a house like that,' he says, 'but I can still dream, can't I?'

Not I. Whether perusing Cotswold-stone farmhouses in an acre of grounds, or flicking through page after page of celebrities, impossibly pert despite the hordes of children trailing in their wake, the net result is the same. It's all unattainable.

I started researching cosmetic surgery. Nothing major, just a tiny tummy tuck to get shot of the baby pouch that resolutely hangs on through diets and fitness regimes, like someone clinging to a tree in a force-ten gale.

I googled dozens of surgeons in my quest to sort out the reputable experts from the chaps in possession of a home-printed certificate and a steak knife. I stood this way and that in front of the mirror, imagining which bits would be lopped off. I became obsessed with how I could save the thousands I needed for the perfect body.

Eventually I decided to confess my plans to my husband. Surely he would understand when he saw how distressed I was about my misshapen midriff? I turned off the television and took a deep breath.

'I'm really unhappy with how I look,' I began. 'It's all I think about, and so I've made a decision.' Rob looked suitably supportive (if a little irked to be missing the rugby), so I ploughed on. 'I want to have some cosmetic surgery.'

'A boob job?' he said immediately. 'It's a big decision, but if that's what you really want—'

'No, not a boob job!' I retorted, almost – but not quite – too affronted to speak. 'Why on earth would you think that?'

He floundered, opening and closing his mouth in what appeared to be a fruitless attempt to turn back time.

'Why would I need a boob job?' I persisted, horrified by the apparent ease with which he had come to this conclusion.

'You don't need a boob job,' he insisted, 'I just assumed—'

'What's wrong with my breasts?' I uncrossed my arms and turned from side to side, thrusting my bosoms towards him like a *Carry On* extra.

'Nothing's wrong with your breasts. I just thought that

if you were going to have surgery, that's what you'd have done.'

The hole my husband was digging was fast approaching epic proportions. Soon he would be needing a rope and crampons to get himself out.

'No,' I replied tersely, 'a boob job is not what I had in mind.' I crossed my arms again, protectively. I am secretly rather proud of my breasts, which – while admittedly not enormous – have to date resisted the pull of gravity, remaining positively enthusiastic and forward-facing.

'Sorry,' he said. There was a pause, during which he wisely decided not to mention my breasts again, and I climbed onto the moral high ground and planted myself firmly there.

My husband adopted an understanding expression. 'Look,' he said, 'I think you're beautiful.'

My heart melted, just a little.

'I love you just the way you are,' he continued, 'and I don't think you need any surgery. But if you feel strongly about it, and you think you would be happier if you had some work done, then I'm not going to stand in your way. We can do some research and see where the best place is.'

Mollified, I nodded and accepted his arms around me.

'Besides,' he said comfortingly, as he stroked my hair. 'It's not about what I, or anyone else thinks, is it? This is about how you feel in yourself. And if a wonky nose is affecting your confidence, then you have every right to do something about it.'

I took a step back. 'Perhaps we could get a buy-one-get-one-free deal – get your nose fixed at the same time as mine.'

He looked confused. 'But my nose is straight.'

'Yes,' I said icily. 'For now.'

MAY

As full of spirit as the month of May.
                                    William Shakespeare

The hawthorn hedges are in full bloom, moth caterpillars valiantly trying to munch their way through the foliage. On the veg patch, with the final frost now safely passed, the ground is soft enough to sow direct, and last year's rhubarb gives you the first crumble of the year. You pass a pleasant hour with a mug of tea and a seed catalogue, committing to carrots and broccoli, and wondering if it's worth giving cucumbers another go. In the fruit bed, strawberries ripen on a layer of straw, although between the birds and the children not a single berry has ever made it as far as the house.

You mourn the loss of your spring-flowering bulbs, but console yourself with the irises you'd forgotten you'd planted. You make hanging baskets for a splash of colour by the front door, and admire the cottage bed that never really had a plan but which has accidentally become quite lovely. Purple geraniums cover the ground, and graceful delphiniums sway in pinks and whites above the blowsy lilac of the hydrangea. You tie up your roses and cut back the lavender, and drag out the garden furniture so you can eat outside.

In the evening, there are bats, swooping on mayflies and squeaking for directions, and you want to wonder at them like everyone else, because you know they are fascinating, and beautiful, and protected. Only you can't forget that story you were told as a child, about the bat entangled in a girl's hair, and so you are secretly relieved when someone says *It's getting a bit chilly, isn't it?* and you can say *Let's take our coffee inside.*

In the daytime, there are swifts, and − although you cannot see him − a cuckoo. It is, of course, a myth that hearing a cuckoo before breakfast will bring ill fortune, but nevertheless you are glad that you have already eaten. He is the first you've heard this spring, and you think about posting something online to see who else has come across one, but it would perhaps be strange among the status updates of lunch choices and cinema check-ins. And besides, there is something rather lovely about thinking you might be the only one to have heard him − that he might be the very first cuckoo of the year − so you stand in the kitchen with the window open, and you keep him all to yourself.

Smuggling children

Disaster fell at the checkout in Sainsbury's at the weekend. I had forgotten my rucksack.

'You can buy a five pence plastic bag or a ten pence bag for life,' the cashier said.

Out of habit, I opted for the bag for life – I'd add it to the three dozen stuffed into the cupboard under the sink at home – but it didn't solve the problem. You can't smuggle snacks into the cinema in a bright orange Sainsbury's bag.

The children groaned, knowing what was coming.

'Not the popcorn, Mummy,' Josh begged. 'It's really scratchy.'

'The drinks, then,' I bargained.

Josh sighed and lifted both trouser legs high enough to enable me to insert a carton of orange juice into each sock.

'They'll fall out!' he said, walking like John Wayne in his efforts to keep them secure.

'Nonsense,' I said briskly. 'It's only for a couple of minutes. Take one for the team, Josh. Right, who's next?'

Manfully, George secreted the scratchy popcorn packet beneath a Manchester City T-shirt, along with strict instructions not to make it rustle by breathing too deeply. Evie took the remaining drinks carton and three packets of fruit pastilles; one up each sleeve and one tucked into her waistband, like a gun-toting sheriff.

'Now,' I instructed as we approached the cinema, 'act natural.'

When I was a teenager the cinema was the default destination for meeting friends on a Saturday, and the obvious choice for a first date. Watching a film was not only an excellent way to mask the fact that my ballet-dancing, book-reading self had little in common with the football-playing, spot-picking products of the boys' grammar, but it was warmer than holding hands at the bus stop and cheaper than a meal at the café. A couple of cinema tickets and a bag of popcorn would set you back no more than a fiver, leaving plenty of pocket money for a copy of *Just Seventeen* and some blue eyeshadow.

Nowadays a new release at the cinema can cost almost a tenner per ticket – not exactly budget-friendly for a big family. Add to that a carton of popcorn and a round of soft drinks and you're looking at an entertainment cost of around a pound a minute. Is it any wonder Netflix is so popular? But much as I love curling up on the sofa for a family film, you can't beat the cinematic experience from time to time, and it is on such occasions I am forced to employ the children as mules.

ONLY FOOD PURCHASED IN THE BUILDING MAY BE CONSUMED, command the many signs fixed to the walls. *THIS IS DUE TO ALLERGIES.*

Ah, allergies, the buzzword of the era. We all know that when restaurants and cinemas play the allergy card they're really playing the we-don't-want-to-lose-any-money card. Because if the risk was that great, we wouldn't be allowed to eat in public at all. Park wardens would be issued powers to take down anyone wielding a ham sandwich, and shopping centre security guards would spend their days hunting down illicit Snickers bars instead of fingering the collars of shoplifters.

I refuse to pay over the odds for less-than-average food, so unless cinemas lower their prices I shall continue to traffic popcorn and orange juice. It has – like many morally dubious activities – become far harder since the children learned to read.

'But it's against the rules,' Evie said piously, poking an errant flash of silver foil back up her sleeve.

'So is letting a nine-year-old watch a film with a twelve certificate,' I replied primly, giving her a knowing glance. She fell obediently back into line as we approached the bored youth taking tickets. I felt my pulse quicken, the way it does when you walk through customs at the airport, despite knowing there's nothing in your luggage except dirty washing and the ill-advised tie-dye kaftan you bought on a whim.

'Mummy,' Evie said urgently, tugging at my sleeve.

'Not now, darling.' I smiled brightly at the sullen youth and handed over our tickets, just as a carton of orange fell audibly out of Evie's sock. She gasped. The youth eyed it suspiciously, as though it might explode.

'You're not allowed to bring food and drink in,' he said.

I bent down to pick up the drink, meeting his gaze full on as I stood up again.

'I have to, I'm afraid,' I told him, in the sort of no-nonsense voice I use when it's bedtime. 'We have allergies.'

At the very mention of the word he took a step back – perhaps in case the allergens in question included excessive hair gel and an over-exuberant use of Sure deodorant – and ushered us inside.

Two can play that game, it seems.

Hill start

It is so much easier to be organised now that practically everything is online. I have just paid my car tax within two minutes of opening the handy reminder that it runs out next month. Gone are the days of queuing at the post office, or waiting for a new disc to arrive in the post and pinning it to the kitchen noticeboard, only for it to slip unnoticed between the skirting board and the bin.

One month, when the children were very little, I realised my car tax expired that very day. The children were baying for their tea and in various states of disarray, their fancy-dress play having been interrupted by my realisation that if I didn't get to the post office *right this second* I wouldn't be able to drive the car over the weekend. With wet weather forecast, the thought of being incarcerated at home for two days with my marauding infants filled me with horror.

I threw the children in the car, put my foot down and hurtled into town, where for once the goddess of parking spaces was smiling on me. There was a space, albeit an illegal one, directly outside the post office. I swerved haphazardly into it and hopped out of the car. Quarter to five. So far, so good. Intending to avoid the kids swarming onto the road, I headed round the front of the car to let them out the other side. Somewhat alarmingly, the car started to roll forward . . . I leapt in front of it and body-slammed the bonnet before it slid into the rather nice Audi in front. With a sinking feeling I realised that in my haste I had neglected to put the handbrake on.

The town is built on a hill, with a car park so steep one requires trekking poles to cross from one side to the other, and I was parked at the top of it. I tentatively inched my way along the bonnet, wondering if I could work up enough speed to reach the handbrake before the car moved too far . . . Not a chance. I was now perilously close to being squashed between my front bumper and the Audi.

The children were getting restless in the back seat and I could see one of them doing something unspeakable. I rapped on the bonnet to get his attention and gave him my infamous stern-mother look. He grinned and carried on. Perhaps I could get him to put the handbrake on? It was worth a try. I began miming to him to take off his seatbelt. He stared at me with his mouth hanging open, making no attempt to undo his belt. Having spent the last year instilling the fear of God into my children in relation to the dangers of taking off their seatbelts, this was perhaps not surprising. I resumed my mime with renewed vigour, stopping only when a passer-by shot me a suspicious glance. It's not every day you see a mother of three performing *Stayin' Alive* dance moves while restraining a fully laden Ford Galaxy.

I should have swallowed my pride and asked him to put on the brake for me. I resolved to ask the next person who came along. I could see a woman at the post-office counter putting her purse back in her bag. She came onto the pavement and headed straight for me with a smile, and with a sinking feeling I realised it was one of the uber-mothers from school.

There was no way I was going to let her see me in such a ridiculous predicament, so I spun round from my spreadeagled position and planted my not-inconsiderable bottom on the bumper, attempting a nonchalant pose as she approached. We passed the time of day until I started to sweat with the exertion of stopping my car from rolling into us.

'Is everything all right?' she asked.

'Not really,' I confessed, admitting my ineptitude and grudgingly asking for help. Uber-Mother nipped to the driver's side and put on the handbrake with a tinkling laugh.

'You are funny, Clare.'

Hilarious.

'It's lucky I was passing,' she continued. 'I just popped in to get a tax disc. It's not due for another month, but it's good to keep it handy on the noticeboard, don't you think?' And with that, she climbed gracefully into the unscathed Audi.

I should have left my car rolling.

Pass the parcel

It appears to be quite the time for post office-related shenanigans.

When you work from home, you become familiar with delivery people. Royal Mail, Hermes, DHL, those UPS chaps who always look faintly embarrassed to be wearing such a terrible uniform . . . they all knock on my door. Occasionally they even have a parcel for me, but most of the time it's for one of our neighbours.

Fellow freelancers complain that such interruptions are the scourge of the work-at-home writer, but taking in a parcel can give my day the sense of purpose it sometimes needs when 'writing a book' has mostly consisted of deleting fifteen thousand words and typing seven new ones. And when Rob comes home from work and asks me how my day has gone, he is far more sympathetic when I explain that I would have surely found my muse had it not been for the delivery of next door's new curtains, and number 38's replacement vacuum cleaner (their third in six months – what do they do with them?). Much better than admitting that, even without external inter-ruptions, I could easily have frittered the day away on social media, or spent an entire morning watching

YouTube videos of kittens falling into bathtubs. (Have you seen them? Really quite hilarious.)

Our regular postal worker is a pleasure to chat to. She's always cheerful, despite Chipping Norton's capacity for sub-zero temperatures when the rest of the Cotswolds are in shorts, and doesn't seem to mind being greeted enthusiastically by a muddy spaniel, who shoots out of the front door like a rat up a drainpipe the second she sees daylight. I have no axe to grind with her. No, this particular axe is destined for 'Royal Mail delivery officer 25', whose red and white missive fluttered through the door at precisely 12.45 this afternoon. I heard the thud of the letterbox and the gentle sound of paper against hall floor, and my heart leaped in the way that it does when the post hasn't yet been, and despite knowing it will only contain bills I can't help but imagine something more exciting, like fan mail, or a film contract for my first book, which stipulates that Benedict Cumberbatch will play the lead, and that he will insist on working very closely with me, in my capacity as writer on set. By the time I had finished imagining the sort of research Mr Cumberbatch might want to carry out I was a little flushed and in need of a peppermint tea.

I went to pick up the post on my way through the hall, and was flabbergasted to see that not only was there not a film contract (with or without Benedict Cumberbatch) but that I was holding in my hands a red and white card informing me that Royal Mail had visited 'while you were out'.

While I was *what*?

While I was ten metres from the front door, in a house with walls so thin you can't put a picture up without a chunk of plaster falling off? [Disclaimer: this may also relate to my DIY skills.] I know I'm knocking on a bit, but I'm fairly confident that either the dog or I would have heard the doorbell ring.

I rang Royal Mail, and spoke to an extremely nice man who logged my complaint and politely informed me that my package (not just a letter, a package! Such anticipation!) could be redelivered in two days.

Two days?

'But what if Benedict needs an answer tomorrow?' I said, before remembering that the mysterious package might not be a film deal after all, and indeed that Benedict Cumberbatch may still be blissfully unaware of my book (this is hard to believe, I know, but he's a busy man, and perhaps not much of a reader).

I put down the phone and tried to get back to work, but the red and white card taunted me from beneath my mug of peppermint tea. If not exciting book news, then what? Delivery officer 25 had confidently ticked the 'it's too large' box, which was promising, although exuberant packaging can be terribly misleading. I once received a pair of swimming goggles in a box large enough to house a television, lovingly swathed in bubble wrap and marked THIS WAY UP.

It was no good, I simply couldn't wait two days; I was going to have to collect it myself. Thus I climbed down from my high horse and into my Ford Galaxy, and drove to the sorting office, to which my parcel had been returned.

'You put this card through the door, *even though I wasn't out*,' I said pointedly, although rather less crossly than on the phone, because after all it wasn't really the man in the sorting office's fault, and also because I really did want my parcel, and I wondered if Royal Mail might have some sort of policy about customer manners.

'Sign here,' the man said. He pushed a dull-looking package across the desk. It wasn't postmarked Hollywood, but perhaps they don't go in for corporate franking machines in LA.

I waited until I was back in the car before tearing open the brown paper, realising almost immediately that my relationship with Benedict Cumberbatch was not yet cemented. Not unless he had taken it upon himself to send me a tray of cinnamon and blueberry muffins, which – let's face it – is unlikely. I mean, how would he even know I liked cinnamon?

I found a card nestling between two slightly squashed muffins.

'Thanks for taking in so many of our parcels,' it read. 'Here's a little something to say sorry for interrupting your work! Best wishes, from number 38.'

Selective breeding

When I was pregnant I consumed how-to manuals in quantities almost as impressive as the jelly and ice cream I craved for six months straight. *What to Expect When You're Expecting* became my bible, supplemented by hundreds of pregnancy magazines, online forums and Facebook pages. I knew everything there was to know about pregnancy, labour, breastfeeding, sleep-training, nappies and weaning.

Such thirst for knowledge had begun years previously, at the beginning of a journey that would ultimately lead to IVF. As anyone to whom babies have not come easily will testify, trying to conceive (ttc, to those in the know) is an all-consuming, seemingly never-ending project over which the participants have limited control. As in pregnancy, knowledge is power. At least that's what you tell yourself.

Eighteen months into Operation Baby, my understanding of menstrual cycles, ovulation and (look away if you're squeamish) cervical mucus would have rivalled that of any gynaecologist. I knew the lifespan of a sperm, every complementary therapy believed to increase chances of success, and the best position to conceive a boy (standing up – you're welcome). I knew *everything*.

Or so I thought.

A decade later and the truth is coming home to roost. There is a key chapter – an entire *section*, indeed – missing from those books on conception. Just as pregnancy books would be more useful focusing less on the birth (which, let's face it, is going to happen regardless of whether you know the right way to breathe) and more on how to cut one's toenails when you can't bend over, so fertility manuals should focus less on the ins and outs of – well, the ins and outs . . . – and more on whether you are attempting to mate with the right person.

I'm not talking about is-he-your-soul-mate-do-you-have-lots-in-common-do-they-hog-the-duvet blah blah blah. I'm not even talking about whether they'll be a good parent. No, this is far more fundamental. And far more useful. It's too late for me, but if you're still at the pre-conception stage, pull up a chair.

Number 1: mate with someone tall.

Not because they make you feel dainty, they're easy to find in shops, and you'll never have to change a light bulb again. Mate with someone tall because five years later (and for sixteen subsequent years) you will not lose several evenings of your life taking up school trousers because you foolishly married someone only five foot two in socked feet.

Now you're getting it, aren't you? Well, listen on – there's more.

Number 2: mate with someone who has zero sporting ability.

Oh, I know it's tempting to have your pick of the front

row, with their cauliflower ears and biceps the size of Bath; and oh goodness, don't those tennis players know what to do with their balls . . . but CONCENTRATE. Focus. Play the long game. Do you really want to spend every Saturday morning shivering by the side of a football pitch? Driving the breadth of the country to watch your progeny compete in a national gymnastics contest? Do you want to wash filthy kit, shell out a fortune for club uniforms, or get roped in to making teas for the cricket club because you may as well – you spend every waking day there anyway?

No, you do not.

Mate with someone with the sporting prowess of an elderly sloth, and you will not have to. [*See also*: musical talent.]

Finally, number three: mate with someone socially inept.

Granted, actually *meeting* someone who struggles to hold a conversation can be a challenge in itself, but one that will more than pay off when your child inherits said social awkwardness and eschews play-dates for the comfort of self-selected solitary confinement. No parental taxis back and forth to friends' houses! No ferrying to youth clubs or waiting outside the school disco at kicking out time! No staying sober because little Johnny needs a lift! Instead: *freedom*.

You see how a little investment early on can pay off?

If you're fortunate enough to still be fertile, free and single, update your Tinder profile and think strategically. *Professional parent-in-waiting seeks mate with no sense of humour and two left feet. Inability to play the piano a plus. Must have own teeth* (there are limits).

Me? I'm currently hovering outside a swimming pool waiting to pick up child number one, then I will deposit her at her BFF's and nip back to take her sibling to guitar, before picking the remaining child up from rugby and going home to take up six pairs of trousers that would otherwise trail in the mud.

It's too late for me, but save yourself. You'll thank me for it.

Secret swinger

Even my own mother, biased though she is, would hesitate to call me sporty. My schooldays passed in a blur of broken hockey sticks and screwed-up PE kits; notes to get out of swimming, and 'could do betters' on my end of term reports. It wasn't so much that I *couldn't* do it – although I have never been gifted with hand-eye coordination – more that I didn't want to. I enjoyed – and was good at – ballet and other forms of dance, but saw nothing pleasurable in standing in the cold in a minuscule netball skirt, waiting for my poor frozen fingers to drop the ball.

On reflection, I blame school entirely for my aversion to sport, and suspect that if they had offered a wider range of options, instead of corralling six hundred girls into netball and hockey, I might have found my niche. As it is, my relationship with exercise will for ever be coloured by memories of giant gym knickers and communal showers.

For a while now, I've secretly wanted to try my hand at golf. A taster session many years ago gave me the bug, and I have harboured a quiet desire to have some lessons and give it a shot ever since. Not only did the injury potential seem far lower than with hockey, but there was something rather civilised about the tradition of having a drink after the eighteenth hole. Rather like après-ski, without the ridiculous panda-eye tan lines. I might have gone for it sooner, had Rob not once made the fatal error of suggesting it.

'You should have a go at golf,' he said, 'then we could play together.'

'I don't think it's really me,' I replied stubbornly. And that was that. My in-laws made several attempts over the years to bring me into the golfing set, but I brushed off their suggestions as laughable. 'A good walk spoiled,' I retorted, quoting someone I always forget.

Then the children started golf lessons.

It happened by chance: a friend of theirs had enjoyed a session at the local club, and there was the possibility of a new class starting, if there were enough children interested. All three of mine liked the idea of it ('We'll be just like Daddy!') and so we trooped up to the golf course on a sunny Saturday morning to hit some balls.

They loved it, and I watched enviously from the side.

'You can join in, if you like,' said the golf pro the following weekend. I like to think he could see untapped potential. 'Or we could organise some private lessons.' That sounded more like it: the children were getting on so well that I suspected I might present rather too amusing a contrast.

'Let's do it,' I said.

I hugged the date to myself as I skipped home. Secret golf lessons. I had everything planned out: I would continue with my lessons until I had an impressive handicap, when I would casually mention to my husband that *Perhaps I'll give this golfing lark a go after all.* We would stroll onto the course, where I might make a play of not knowing how to hold my club ('Could you show me, darling?') before teeing off with panache and sending the ball three hundred yards onto the green. Cue an amazed husband, and perhaps a smattering of light applause from the players waiting behind us.

My first lesson was hard going, but I wasn't disheartened. Rome wasn't built in a day. Lessons two and three passed, and then four and five. Was this the most frustrating game ever?

'How long before I'll actually be able to play a game?' I asked my ever-patient teacher. He sighed, taking in the mound of divots collecting at my feet.

'A few more weeks,' he said. 'Maybe.'

On my sixth lesson I collected my first injury, when I misjudged my downswing and hit the ground with enough force to send a jolt of pain into my hand.

'Are you okay?' Rob asked that evening, when I was forced to use my left hand to lift the kettle.

'Yes!' I winced. 'Nothing to worry about.' I thought about giving up, but the same stubbornness that had seen me refuse to pick up a golf club for years now stopped me from chucking in the towel. It dawned on me that if I were to wait until I had a respectable handicap before hustling my husband, that one or both of us could well be in a bath chair.

I decided to come clean.

'That's fantastic!' Rob said, with genuine admiration. 'Well done you.'

He came with me for some practice swings, and I braced myself for a repeat of our tennis debacle. But time had mellowed either him or me, and I managed not to bristle at his offers of help, achieving some semi-respectable shots.

'Might be a while before I can join you for a game,' I said ruefully.

'Oh, I don't know,' he said. 'I think you're a natural.'

Let them eat brioche

I went downstairs this morning to find Rob and Josh sitting opposite each other in stony silence, a look of mirrored mutiny between them.

'What on earth's happened?' I asked, assuming a calamity of epic proportions.

'There isn't any brioche,' sighed Josh, 'and Daddy's eaten the last croissant.' He held up a piece of toast between resentful fingers and eyed it balefully. 'So I have to eat *this.*' He may as well have been presented with a plate of live worms, for the complete disdain on his face.

'Oh for heaven's sake,' I said, 'it's all bread, isn't it?'

My miniature food critic rolled his eyes and shook his head sadly, munching reluctantly on his slice of wholemeal toast. I am clearly a hopeless case when it comes to dough-related matters.

The situation, of course, is one of my own making. Had I not introduced the children to breakfasts of honeyed crumpets, poached eggs on muffins, waffles, pancakes, croissants and brioche, they would have been none the wiser. But I have embraced our well-stocked supermarkets and in doing so broadened my children's culinary tastes.

I'm not alone: a quick straw poll among my friends

reveals my choice of menu is a sign of the times. When I was young breakfast was a bowl of heavily sugared cornflakes and a Ski yoghurt. Now it's all granola and home-made smoothies. It's giving children airs above their station.

The problem manifested itself early on, when a then-six-year-old Evie threw a tantrum in Sainsbury's. She had needled me from the moment she spotted her target on the shelf. 'Oh please may we have some? Oh pleeeease, Mummy, pleeeease . . .' When that didn't work she stamped her feet and crossed her arms across her chest. 'Put it in the trolley now!' she ordered, desperation making her voice quiver. Finally she hurled herself to the floor and wept copiously as I stepped over her to reach the deli counter.

I was terribly embarrassed, but not because she was having a tantrum. I was mortified because it wasn't sweets she was screaming for, or chips, or chocolate biscuits. All these would have earned me a look of solidarity from other mothers; after all, who hasn't given in to pleas for sweet treats in the supermarket? But no, my daughter was after the organic falafel.

'Mummy, PLEASE! Please can we have faffafel?'

Middle-class tantrums are on a whole different level.

A combination of television advertising, our own eclectic menu and a host of friends with equally wide-ranging diets means that for years now my children have taken an irritatingly keen interest in the provenance of our meals. With even Captain Birdseye's media men in on the act, the kids have been prone to sanctimonious questioning just as I'm dishing up.

'Are these fish fingers sustainably sourced, Mummy?' they'd pipe as I handed round their plastic plates. Since the fingers in question were ninety-nine pence from one of those four-letter supermarkets, I very much doubted they were. In fact I was rather dubious they contained fish at all.

'Of course, darling.' I smiled sweetly, dolloping mashed potato onto their plates. 'The haddock is line-caught by fishermen paid a fair wage for their toils. In fact,' I said, warming to my theme, 'even the breadcrumbs are sustainable.'

Years later, with my children's dietary habits long ingrained, I yearn for a time when mothers could serve up defrosted chicken Kievs, boil-in-the-bag rice and anything from a tin. When it was perfectly acceptable to have just one vegetable with your casserole, instead of at least three (of which at least one will have arrived in the Riverford box that afternoon and required you to *look it up on the internet* before you could cook it).

Yesterday the children had a friend over for tea. I made pizza dough and spread the resulting base liberally with home-made passata. I tore mozzarella into pieces and scattered garden herbs across the top. I swore my way through thirty chunky-cut potato chips, tossed them in olive oil and baked them crispy. The tribe fell ravenously on their supper and it wasn't long before the doorbell rang for our guest to be collected.

'Did you eat your supper nicely?' asked his mother.

'We had pizza and chips!' the boy announced gleefully.

'Well, actually . . .' I began, but faltered immediately.

Well, actually it was home-made? Well, actually the cheese was organic? Well, actually I can cook, honestly – I didn't just throw a frozen pizza in the oven? Oh, what's the point? 'He ate it all beautifully,' I confirmed, and we waved as our well-fed guest and his mother drove away.

So this morning I had little patience for children looking down their noses at a breakfast which didn't involve pain au raisin, or pain au chocolat, or pain au something else. I rummaged in the back of the larder and pulled out a box of cornflakes. Reaching for the milk, I poured him a generous bowl, topped with sugar.

'Tuck into these,' I said. 'They're sustainably caught flakes of organic corn. I think you'll like them.'

And he did.

Where children lie

The graveyard is still and quiet, no matter what time of the year I visit. The church sits squarely in the centre, its heavy oak doors never locked, and few sounds to interrupt those seeking sanctuary. A cobbled path meanders past the church, between ancient chest tombs and gravestones too weather-worn to read. Years ago I would run through these monuments, racing late to school with my mother as the church bell rang nine, the hidden histories of the churchyard nothing more than a playground to me.

On my wedding day, in that same place, I smiled to think of that four-year-old girl. I picked my way on silver heels across uneven ground, holding tight to my father's arm and giving no more thought to the ancient headstones than which would provide the best backdrop for our photographs.

I didn't see the children's garden.

I didn't even know it was there.

I must have walked past it a thousand times without so much as a glance. It occupies a corner of the churchyard beneath an enormous pine tree, branches reaching out to cover each of its charges. The ducks in the pond swim past with a seemingly endless stream of fluffy duck-lings, and I am at once comforted by this reminder of new life and pained to see it so close to the rows of tiny headstones, each name framed by a bracket of time so impossibly short.

Today I sit beside my son and clear the weeds that stubbornly creep across the rectangle of ground I am equally determined to keep clear. I need to see the earth; I can't bear to think of the grass closing in and shutting me off. Now I can place my hand flat on the ground, the damp earth pulling at my skin, and know he is just beneath me. Almost touching me.

I tip the rainwater from the little metal vase and fetch fresh water from the dripping tap in the corner of the churchyard. I cut short the yellow roses that are really too big for such a small grave, and replace the vase in the base of the stone. His headstone is simple: a square of white marble, the lettering picked out with gilt that shines as I rub a cloth over it to remove the lichen and fallen pine needles.

I work methodically, feeling lighter as the grime comes away and the stone is once again clean and bright. I don't talk to him – at least, not out loud, not in the way I see others doing, their lips moving as they stand beside well-tended graves.

Instead I think.

I think about how I should be tidying his bedroom, not his grave, despairing at the Lego figures scattered across the floor, the balled-up socks under the bed. I think about what he'd be doing at school, whether he'd be musical, good at sport, kind to animals. I think about how much his twin brother misses him. How much I miss him.

Sometimes, as I sit beside his grave, I rail inside at the injustice of it all, screaming silently at a world that lets children die. But mostly I test out my grief. I open it up, just a little, in the way you probe a sore tooth, to see if it's still there. To see if time has healed. It never has, of course. Even that tiny chink releases a bolt of pain which knocks me sideways, the familiar tightness forming in my chest and closing my throat until each breath is an effort.

Today, someone has left a small pewter angel by the side of his grave.

I didn't put it there, and the flowers of those who visit regularly are never accompanied by anything more permanent. Looking around, I see there is one next to every grave. Two dozen tiny angels, placed with care to watch over our babies.

It doesn't matter to me who put them there: it is enough to know that there are people who care about these lost children, when so often it feels the world has forgotten. I say a silent goodbye and leave my son playing with the other boys and girls, safe beneath the outstretched arms of the pine tree, in our quiet corner of the churchyard.

JUNE

I wonder what it would be like to live in a world where it was always June.

L. M. Montgomery

Summer! The best part of summer, at that, when another three months of sunshine are still entirely possible, and the hordes of tourists haven't yet made it impossible to park anywhere near the shops. You trade the pleasure of bare legs in shorts with the risk of nettles on the footpaths, and spend half your walk hunting for dock leaves to ease the stinging.

The long evenings and the scent of wild honeysuckle lure you into walking longer, later. You lean on a wall to watch the farmers making hay, enthralled by the baling machine, and sneezing at the dust thrown up when it passes you.

In the garden, you give up on your brassicas. You have spent diligent days checking the nets, and scraping clutches of white eggs from the underside of the leaves, but every plant is a mass of tiny caterpillars. You are incapable of crossing the garden without stopping to pinch out a weed, deadhead a rose, or fling a snail away from the strawberries, and you wish you could spend the whole day pottering.

You wait for a warm, dry day, and take your basket to the edge of the woods, where the elder is just starting to flower. You will make cordial in old-fashioned bottles, and tell yourself how much better it is for you than shop-bought juices, even though the sugar you pour into the pan makes your teeth itch. Come Christmas, the children will drink it diluted with water; the grown-ups will add theirs to glasses filled with crushed ice and mint leaves, lime juice and prosecco. They will make a toast, and you will be happy that you spent that precious Saturday infusing elderflower, and straining it through muslin into the wide pan that used to be your mother's.

There are barbecues, where the women make salads and the men stand around open flames, watching sausages turn from pink to black, and no one cares because everything tastes wonderful when it's eaten by a fire. There are garden games of badminton and swingball, and croquet with the set you lost a hoop from two summers ago. There are complaints from the children that they *can't go to bed yet – it's still light!* and half-hearted insistence from their parents, who remember too well that need to wring every last moment from the day.

You remember it, too. You remember that when you were a child the summer seemed to last for ever, and that it is only as you became an adult that the days began to race. And so you shrug, and you let bedtime slide, and you make the most of the glorious month of June.

The naked truth

I have left the leisure centre. The whole showering with strangers thing was just too awkward, and the near miss with the swim club was the final straw. My new gym is a private health club, where the uniforms are white and monogrammed, like in a luxury spa, and every piece of equipment has a TV and internet access.

Not that I use the equipment much, since the swimming pool is blissfully quiet and surrounded by neat rows of loungers on which to read a book or grab forty winks, before heading for the changing rooms where there are – such bliss! – *private showers*.

There are two breeds of women in swimming-pool changing rooms: those who divest themselves of their swimsuit beneath a wrapped towel, and those who shouldn't be permitted to use swimming-pool changing rooms. If you're the sort of person who likes to prance about public changing rooms with your maracas swaying, I'm afraid you and I are not going to get on.

Don't get me wrong: I'm no prude. I left my dignity in the doctor's waiting room the day the question of my fertility arose, and I never got round to going back for it. Since then I've had enough consultants rummaging around my nether regions to make a glove puppet blush, with motherhood itself putting paid to any grandiose ideas about privacy. I don't think I've had a bath on my own since 2006, and lately I've taken to crossing my legs till the children go off to school in the morning, just so I can have an uninterrupted wee.

In a small house with two adults, three children and a busy schedule there's no place for modesty. Bathroom doors are left open, naked children streak across the landing (grown-ups too, from time to time, given enough Sauvignon Blanc), and no one bats an eyelid at what George so charmingly calls Mummy's wobbly bits.

That's all fine: we're family, after all. But the lady at the gym who saunters from the shower to the locker? I don't know her from Eve, yet I'm more intimate than I could ever want to be with the two-inch tattoo of a seahorse above her left nipple. Would it really be too much to ask to use a towel?

I'm not suggesting there should be no nudity at all – it would make changing room rather a misnomer, after all – but putting on a pair of pants is easier than doing the hokey-cokey. You put your left leg in, your right leg in . . . and pull them up. Job done, modesty preserved. Why this obsession with getting fresh air to your nether regions? Find a corner and get your undercrackers on, and only then should you be allowed to mosey around drying your hair and making the most of the free hand cream.

Such gay abandon was never a problem at the leisure centre, where the freezing temperatures and the tangle of wet hair on the floor meant no one was tempted to linger for long. It never occurred to me that in pursuing a more luxurious fitness experience (and complimentary fluffy towels) I would find myself making friends on a more gynaecological level than is generally sought by those of us of a heterosexual persuasion.

One of the more uninhibited women at my health club is particularly chatty. Believe me when I tell you this is an uncomfortable combination. Politeness dictates a certain level of eye contact when someone is speaking to you, but have you ever tried to discuss the Sky News headlines with a woman in the buff? I can assure you it's most disconcerting. Chatty naked woman gaily shares her theories on everything from terrorism to MPs' expenses as she gets dressed, meaning she is frequently halfway through a sentence when she turns round and bends over to dry her toes, planting her damp buttocks inches from my face. Frankly I think I preferred the carpet of wet hair at the leisure centre.

I have come to the conclusion there is only one way to address the issue: to locate the thermostat and turn it down a few notches. Admittedly I won't have quite the luxurious experience I have enjoyed up till now, but with any luck the resulting icy temperature will encourage people to cover up, meaning I'll see more fluffy white towels, and fewer bottoms.

The long arm of the law

Last month I was caught speeding. Yes, yes, how ironic for an ex-copper. But, just like dentists need crowns, and doctors come down with the occasional sniffle, we former law-enforcers are not entirely above reproach.

I won't linger on the fact that it was practically the middle of the night when I got caught, and nowhere near a school and honestly, I was only doing 35 in a 30 . . . (although all those things are true), because ultimately – it's a fair cop. I broke the law.

I was caught by a camera, not a real-life police officer, which was a shame as it robbed me of the opportunity to flutter my eyelashes and offer unmentionable bribes in the hope he would let me off. It's probably just as well, as all I had left in my handbag by the end of the day was a twenty-pence piece and an emergency Crunchie bar, and I'd have been reluctant to let the chocolate go, just in case.

Because of the really very slow speed I was doing (only 35 in a 30, did I mention?) I was offered a choice: take the sixty-pound fine and the accompanying three points, or attend a speed awareness course for the princely sum of ninety pounds. You know the sort of thing: an educational alternative to prosecution, which has the advantage of enabling you to renew your car insurance without crossing your fingers behind your back when you're asked if your licence is clean. The purpose of speed awareness courses is to show people the error of their ways, so they leave at lunchtime vowing to never again exceed the speed limit.

It doesn't work, of course.

I know this because this will, in fact, be the third speed awareness course I have been on. You see, although the courses are aimed at first-time offenders, it seems you can 'first-time offend' once every three years. And furthermore, you can 'first-time offend' in different counties. This is excellent for those of us in the Cotswolds, where a twenty-minute school run can dip into three different counties. So, despite the promising blurb on the speed awareness website, which assures me the course will improve my driving, my ability to read the road and my awareness of my fellow road-users, I remain cynical. Because experience tells me I will spend four hours in a room with nineteen other disgruntled and resentful individuals, introducing ourselves and our offences, and doing 'fun' questionnaires about speed limits. It's like a cross between a bad pub quiz and Alcoholics Anonymous.

I've been swotting up on my Highway Code, so that I can correctly answer questions about stopping distances in a bored manner, while leaning back in my chair and examining my nails. It's a technique several of us adopted in sixth form, when revising was simply not the Done Thing, but at the same time we were secretly rather keen to get into university because of all the boys and the drugs and the louche living we'd been promised (none of which ever materialised). My friend Sally and I used to stay up for hours studying, then pretend our ashen faces and perpetual yawns were down to pulling an all-nighter at Ritzy's nightclub. It worked like a charm; we secured our As and Bs, yet kept our street cred. I'm hopeful I can still pull off the cool look.

That's assuming I can make it on time: I was dismayed to see that the speed awareness course starts at 9 a.m. sharp. (In fact, I see from the joining instructions we are encouraged to arrive at 8.45 a.m. for 'tea and coffee with your fellow participants'. Gosh, that sounds like fun.) I can't put the kids on the school bus till 8.40, so I'm not sure how I'm going to make the twenty-mile journey by nine.

I guess I'll just have to put my foot down.

Slim pickings

Is there anything more depressing than dieting? The prospect of lunch normally carries me through even the busiest of mornings, and when I am finding it hard choosing the words to put down on the page, a quick trip to the fridge is a welcome distraction. But I can find nothing enticing about today's offering of Ryvita and cottage cheese, and everything seems harder to write without a cup of milky coffee and a KitKat.

The crux of the matter is that food isn't simply nutrition, is it?

It tastes good, it makes us feel good, and it's linked to so many enjoyable activities. Coffee and a slice of cake with a good friend, Sunday lunch with the family, a romantic dinner à deux when a babysitter's been booked. Food lies at the heart of everything, so dieting sweeps through all the fun stuff in life and replaces it with bland flavours, hunger pangs and an empty diary.

Blessed with good genes and a fast metabolism, I skipped through my teens without so much as a sniff of puppy fat, and stayed an effortless size ten throughout my twenties, despite a diet consisting mostly of kebabs and cheap cider. I remember my mother looking at herself in the mirror and bemoaning the loss of her waist.

'I was always so slim,' she sighed.

Privately I thought she must be viewing the past through rose-tinted glasses: surely one didn't simply morph from a naturally slim figure to a fuller one.

Oh, how naïve I was . . .

Somewhere after thirty, when I was busy chasing children and looking the other way, someone snuck in and replaced my runaway burger-and-chips metabolism with one unable to process so much as a Hobnob without it appearing on my thighs within seconds. The merest sniff of a sausage roll is enough to send the scales into orbit, and so, despite my conviction at the start of the year that I would never resolve to give up food, I have reluctantly joined the ranks of professional dieters.

I'm not one for support groups. You can rave all you want about Slimming World and Weight Watchers, but public weigh-ins aren't for me. Peer support is all well and good, but if I unwrap an illicit Twix as I walk down the high street, I don't want some do-gooder popping out of the post office to 'help me stay on track'. No, when I diet, I do it on my terms. There was the cabbage soup diet (disastrous for anyone following downwind), the juice diet (brilliantly effective, but very expensive) and the 5:2 diet, which started well, then gradually became the 6:1 diet, and then . . . well, you know.

I blame the children. Not just for triggering my middle-aged spread, but for making it impossible to avoid temptation. The biscuit tin is always full, the fridge groans with lunchbox niceties like mini cheeses and German sausage, and everyone knows it's impossible to clear a table without hoovering up the leftover fish fingers.

What I really need is a version of the child-proof seals found on aspirin bottles: adult-proof locks on anything containing tasty food, leaving only the lettuce leaves and crispbreads within my grasp.

I'm back to the basics this time around: eating less, moving more. The dog is still in shock after our post-school-run ramble turned into a three-mile route march, and the car sits forlornly on the drive as I staunchly ignore its comfort and trek up the hill into town. With a half-hour walk equalling one glass of wine, never has there been more of an incentive to get moving.

Like giving up smoking, going public with one's dieting plans is fraught with risk. On the one hand, telling people you're watching your weight makes it easier to stick to your guns; on the other, the whole world is there to see you stuff doughnuts in your mouth when you've had a bad day. Right now, at the end of week one, I'm feeling good. A couple of pounds down, chocolate cravings under control – what could possibly go wrong?

But, like all good intentions, I know my resolve will weaken over the next few weeks, and I'll once again be reaching for the biscuit tin. So if you see me in the queue at the Chinese takeaway, or tweeting about a decadent dinner, let's both do the decent thing and pretend you never read this.

Guardian angels

Rob and I have recently adopted the survival strategy historically favoured by the Royal Family. We travel separately: we never sit in the same railway carriage and take two cars on long journeys. Have we been arguing? Do we have a surplus of funds to splash out on travel expenses? Perhaps we have misunderstood the raging environmental debate and pledged to *enlarge* our carbon footprint?

None of the above. We have simply been embroiled for several weeks now in a discussion about what would happen to the children in the event of our simultaneous death. A macabre thought, I know, and admittedly the odds are slim, but then so were the odds of having two sets of twins, so I don't set much store by statistics.

An only child is pretty easy to place – all your friends and family jump at the chance to act *in loco parentis*, so you can have your pick of possibilities. After all, everyone's got space for just one more.

'Be his guardian? Oh we'd be honoured!' was the reaction from Josh's godparents as they cradled our three-month-old son in their arms. (Top tip: identify and ask prospective guardians when your baby is still small, cute and largely inoffensive. If you wait till he becomes a threenager before attempting to palm him off on relatives, you may find stair-gates slammed in your face. For similar reasons, it's best to target couples who haven't themselves yet taken the plunge into parenthood. Once they've got their own rug rat to worry about, the prospect of taking on someone else's becomes significantly less attractive.)

Less than a year after our successful conversation with the first set of godparents, two more babies arrived on the scene and the issue of guardianship became rather more thorny. With the possible exception of Angelina Jolie, who has room in their lives for an extra three children? Come to that, who has space in their house? The children may have been quite little at the time, but I confidently predicted they'd grow.

I wondered if it might be best to split up the brood and dish out a child to each willing family, perhaps devising some sort of timeshare in the unlikely event I found more than three prospective guardians. Except that the children might need each other – while it's true they have probably already had their fill of the screaming banshee that presents as their mother, I flatter myself that they would be somewhat traumatised by my passing, and be glad of one another's support.

I suppose we could have approached our mothers – after all, they did a decent enough job bringing us up. But grandparents today are a far cry from the white-haired, toffee-sucking figures of my youth. My mother-in-law is in the gym every day and my own mother gallivants around the country on theatre tours. Being saddled with three grandchildren would rather cramp their style.

Unbeknown to my friends I've been working on a couple of likely candidates for guardianship. I have surreptitiously inspected their homes for suitable accommodation and made a rough assessment of their financial situation based on their annual holiday and supermarket of choice. The next step is to make them fall in love with the children. Each time we visit I make sure to dress them with particular care, combing hair and tying it with ribbons, and removing any trace of unidentified substances from noses and hands. Placid smiles result from a hissed bribe of chocolate, and the soporific effect of a precautionary dose of Calpol.

Such behaviour has been unfailingly met with compliments: 'So beautifully behaved, what a joy they are, how lovely, how precious, how delightful!'

I'm biding my time until the moment's right to follow up the compliments with 'Yes, aren't they – would you like one of them?'

In the meantime we have adopted the time-honoured tactic of total avoidance. We reduce the likelihood of a joint accident by never going anywhere together, and avoid discussing it further for fear that the stress may cause us to spontaneously combust.

Because then who would look after the children?

The unstealable spaniel

When I was young, the noticeboard in the village would occasionally play host to a Lost Dog poster. 'Beloved pet,' it would read, 'reward offered for safe return.' My sister and I would spend the weekends *Just William*-style, fruitlessly hunting back gardens for lost labs in the hope of earning ourselves the promised fortune. We never got lucky, but then there were never very many dogs to find: perhaps one or two throughout a long, hot summer that tipped gently into autumn, the new school term leaving little time for bounty hunting.

Nowadays you can't move without seeing a similar plea, the owner's anguish as tangible as if each mass-produced poster were hand-streaked with tears. On my daily dog walk across fields and through woods I might encounter half a dozen of these home-made appeals, each with the name of the dog emblazoned beneath its photo: Freddie, Buster, Sally.

Back home, browsing Facebook when I should be working, a dozen more images are pushed to my feed. BEWARE DOG-NAPPERS! The thefts are rife: spaniels stolen, rare Pekinese lured from old ladies walking in the park, puppies physically snatched from young owners introducing them to the lead for the first time.

Have there always been so many dog thieves around? Were the lost dogs of my childhood summers not lost at all, but thrown into white vans to be sold on? Even allowing for the scaremongering so easily perpetuated by the internet, the rise in reported cases is worrying.

As a result, I have become a cautious owner: Maddie is not only microchipped and identity-tagged, but has a second tag sewn into the underside of her collar in case the first is removed. Although I'll allow her to romp off the lead, she never leaves my sight, and should we walk anywhere close to a road I keep her safely by my side. It's not the traffic I fear, but the fabled white van, driven by men who seem to be able to grab a dog then disappear without a trace. What do they do with the dogs? Who buys them? Are they sold for pets – the best-case scenario, I suppose – or sacrificed as fighting dogs, no more significant than a pound of meat? My paranoia is heightened by the number of spaniels believed stolen – far more than pugs or terriers, or any of the other hundreds of breeds.

'Gun dogs,' my friend Charlotte tells me knowledgeably, after another brace of springers disappears from kennels at a farm up the road. 'They steal trained dogs, which can then be sold on for big money.'

Instinctively, I look around for Maddie, who has her muzzle thrust into the warm centre of a cow pat and is swallowing enthusiastically.

Charlotte looks awkward. 'Um, I think you're safe.'

'What do you mean?' I say. How could any dog-napper

resist my lovable adolescent spaniel? I call her and she bounds off in the opposite direction, where a rotting bird provides the canine equivalent of a tub of Ben & Jerry's.

'We-ll,' Charlotte says tentatively, 'she's not exactly well trained, is she?'

As if to illustrate the point, Maddie ignores my command to drop the dead bird, instead bringing it to me and dancing around as though I might be persuaded to play fetch with its putrid body.

I sigh. 'No, I guess she isn't.' The truth of the matter is that, despite my best intentions, I have failed miserably to train my dog beyond the basics, and even those basics are liable to be abandoned in favour of an interesting smell, the neighbour's cat, or anyone carrying something that might contain biscuits.

The biddable dog I had envisaged when I first started puppy-training – that dog who waited meekly by my side, nose brushing my knee with every step I took – is so far removed from my hyperactive companion it's laughable. On cue, Maddie jumps up at me, leaving muddy footprints on my stomach. I catch my friend's eye.

'She's not that bad,' I say.

There's a pause.

'She is. But look on the bright side: at least she's unlikely to be dog-napped.'

I wipe at my coat, realising too late that the brown sticky substance isn't mud after all. I glare at Maddie, for a split second entertaining the idea of clothes without dog hair, a house without mud . . .

Then she looks at me with her head on one side, and her mouth slightly open, big brown eyes telling me that − dead birds aside − I mean the whole world to her.

I lean down and ruffle her ears. Man's best friend: isn't that what they say?

The committee compulsion

It wasn't long into my time as a school-run mum before I was strong-armed onto the PTA. I had deposited a five-year-old at the classroom door and was heading for the school gate when I heard the unmistakable clomp of Joules wellies running to catch up with me. 'Hello!' came the call, lest I failed to stop at the sound of her heavy tread, 'Josh's mum!' (First names become irrelevant once you have children, particularly if you don't have a job to go to during school hours. You're either so-and-so's wife or so-and-so's mother. It's terribly irritating.) I pinned a smile on my face and turned to greet the panting woman behind me.

'Hello,' I said, 'you're Rachel's mother, aren't you?' (Ah yes, I see the irony here. Perhaps I should make some name badges.)

'That's right. I'm so glad I caught you. I wanted to ask if you could possibly find some time to come along to the next PTA meeting. We've had a bit of a shake-up recently and there are some really exciting opportunities.'

This, of course, is code for *the entire committee has bailed and we're desperate for someone to run the summer fête.* My heart sank. I was up to my eyeballs in work, co-organiser of a literary festival and on two fundraising groups. I simply didn't have the time for yet another committee.

'Of course,' I heard myself saying. 'I'd love to.'

And that was the moment at which I realised I had turned into my mother. In many respects, this is no bad thing. My mother is an extremely nice woman. But she is incapable of saying no to anything, and I appear to have inherited the gene. Whether it's baking for the cake stall, taking on an impossible deadline or joining a new committee, I find myself nodding enthusiastically and shoehorning another evening meeting into my diary. Last month I ran a fundraising stall at the theatre at the same time as attending a committee meeting in the pub next door. I legged it between venues at quarter-hour intervals, swigging gin and craning to read the secretary's minutes to see what I'd missed. Not a lot, as it turned out, although that might have been because I was supposed to have been chairing the meeting.

Aside from my mother's genes, I have no idea why I have such a compulsion to join committees. I don't even like committees. I particularly dislike committees full of women. I know that's a terribly non-PC thing to say, but in my experience meetings made up of men are blissfully uncomplicated. Blokes get straight down to business, whip through the agenda and bang out actions like they're dealing cards. Meetings always – but *always* – finish in time for last orders.

In stark contrast, their female counterparts may optimistically suggest a start time of 7.30 p.m., but the first half-hour at least is given over to sympathetic chat about idle husbands, misbehaving infants, and the mythical work/life balance. Those of us wise to this pattern tend to arrive late, hoping to miss the tittle-tattle and cut straight to the chase. Unfortunately, as so many committee members feel the same way, all that happens is that everyone arrives late and the half-hour preamble runs till 8.30 p.m. Each agenda item will then be debated, every view listened to and responded to with appropriate care, each prompting a tangent so lengthy it is sometimes impossible to drag the discussion back to its original point.

Such diplomacy is admirable, and women do seem to be particularly brilliant at making people feel good about themselves, but all this tact is so terribly time-consuming. I can't help but feel the guys have it right: any less-than-ideal suggestion is simply met with a 'Bloody stupid idea, Jim!' and a round of raucous laughter. It's possible that poor Jim slinks home afterwards to drown his sorrows in three fingers of whisky, but I suspect he simply shrugs it off and moves on.

Dish out the same response to the female committee member who proposes doing away with the coconut shy at the summer fête, and it'll be floods of tears and a resignation before you can say 'There, there.'

Perhaps I should try to establish the gender balance of a committee before allowing myself to be co-opted. A testosterone level lower than 50 per cent and I bail?

I haven't got time to think about it now. I've got a committee meeting to get to.

JULY

The summer looks out from her brazen tower,
Through the flashing bars of July.

Francis Thompson

The lawn is dry and brown, and it's been weeks since you carried a jacket *just in case*. You know that this weather can't last, but oh . . . what if it did? What if the summer stretched through September, if it was all ice creams and salads, and trips to the beach? What if it was rolling down hills, and walks with the dog, and never checking the forecast?

Hollyhocks cast shadows through your windows, growing taller than you ever imagined, and recklessly you cut some for a vase you fill with phlox and cow parsley, foxgloves and the last of the lupins. Now you have a cottage garden in your kitchen, too, and the scent is heady and intoxicating. It hasn't rained for three weeks, and you keep one eye on the sprinkler, and the other on the headlines, waiting for the hosepipe ban that comes every year.

As the coachloads of tourists have grown, expelling their camera-keen contents onto pavements too narrow to hold them, so you have stayed away. You have not been to the rivers in Bibury and Bourton, or to the Slaughters, or to Stroud. You have been instead to the lavender fields at Broadway, catching them at harvest, and filling a basket in the shop with scented creams and bags of lavender grain you will keep in your bedroom drawers. You have walked around the Rollright Stones, and counted a different number every time, just as legend has it. You have been to Wychwood Wild Garden, to where the pond hides within the trees, and kept the dog from chasing the ducks. You have been to Blenheim Palace, where two thousand acres mean there is always a quiet spot somewhere. You have kept these corners of the Cotswolds to yourself, and you have enjoyed them all the more for it.

Getting the chop

I've been with my hairdresser for a long time. I met her at a salon when we moved to Chipping Norton, and she's been cutting my hair ever since. When she left, to work for herself as a mobile stylist, I left too, swapping the luxury of the salon for my kitchen chair (and saving myself a pretty penny into the bargain). We get on well, she and I. I like her, and I think she likes me. We talk lots and we've never had an argument. But there's no way round it: lately our relationship has got a little stale. She knows what I like, and she gives it to me. Where's the excitement? Where's the thrill? It's all just a little bit predictable. I couldn't help but wonder if there was something more . . .

I found myself looking at other women's hair, wondering where they'd had it cut. Was their stylist more adventurous than mine? Did they get a head massage when they had their hair washed? Were they offered Earl Grey and a biscuit? However much I tried to be loyal, I couldn't help my thoughts drifting towards something new. Something different. Something exciting.

The next time she came round to give me a trim, I could hardly look her in the eye. Should I tell her I'd been looking elsewhere? Confess to my wandering eye?

I wondered if honesty really was the best policy: would it be the making of us? The catalyst we needed, to give our relationship another go? But I just couldn't bring myself to do it. How could I tell her she wasn't enough for me, after so many years together? So I told her about my holiday, and she asked about the kids, and all the time I was imagining lying back in a leather recliner, with someone else's fingers running through my hair.

'Are you okay?' she said. 'You seem a little distracted.'

'I'm fine,' I muttered, blushing so badly my highlights turned red.

She knew: I was sure of it.

Thoughts of infidelity became an obsession. I donned dark glasses and popped into salons to pick up price lists, taking furtive looks around me as I emerged, terrified I'd be spotted. I contemplated heading out of town, to where no one knew me: I'd heard of a place where they gave free samples of shampoo in beautiful linen bags, and became convinced such products would revolutionise my hair.

But I didn't do it. I never crossed that line.

Then the new salon opened in town.

Sleek. Elegant. Expensive. I heard word the owner came from London, that they served cocktails, that their chairs were imported from Japan, and made from the softest leather. I walked past once, twice. I flirted with them on Twitter.

Then I booked an appointment.

It was as easy as that, but even as I took the appointment card and stroked its Cotswold-green lettering, I wondered if I could go through with it. I imagined what my old hairdresser would say – how she would feel . . .

I pushed the thought aside. I wanted adventure. Excitement.

I wanted shiny hair.

I woke this morning with adrenalin coursing through my veins. I wore a new dress and red lipstick – could hardly wait to drop the kids at school and get to the salon.

It was everything I had imagined.

A glass of champagne sailed towards me as gentle hands explored my hair and the hairdresser threw out phrases such as 'beautiful colouring', 'lovely length', and 'very badly damaged – have you been dyeing this yourself?' (Reader, I had.)

And then it was upstairs to the basins, where I lay back and shivered with pleasure: not at the touch of my colourist, but at the contrast to my own toothpaste-encrusted, odd-sock-strewn bathroom. Such bliss! Such happiness!

Such . . . guilt.

The remorse began at my follicles and ended at the tips of my fingers, which twisted themselves in my lap in shame. Back in the cutting chair, my champagne forgotten, I chewed my lip and stared at the gargantuan gilt mirror before me.

At the face of a cheat.

How could I do this to my lovely hairdresser? Sure, I'd have great hair, but *she* gave me great hair! And what were a few shampoo samples, if it meant the end of our relationship?

I reached for my phone. I couldn't live with the guilt

– I had to tell her. I tapped out a text message, pouring out my confession, and begging her to forgive me.

'It's not you, it's me,' I said. 'I was thinking of you all the time . . .'

Text message sent, I waited anxiously for the fall-out.

It came quickly. 'Is that the new guy from London? I've heard great things – let me know what it's like!'

Was that it? Was I so easily forgotten?

I choked back a sob.

'More champagne?' my new hairdresser asked.

'Bring the bottle,' I said.

Bargain hunt

I once queued outside Next in the centre of Oxford, on a freezing cold Boxing Day morning. At 6 a.m. there were already a dozen people in the queue, and when the doors opened at nine we were trampled underfoot by the fifty or so sharp-elbowed shoppers who had arrived after us. Inside, you couldn't move for bargain-hunters. Clothes were torn from hangers, held up hopefully, then discarded or shoved unceremoniously into baskets. The canniest shoppers didn't pause to try things on, or spend more than a second assessing an item's potential: they scanned the rail with a practised eye, plucking out this top, those trousers, that swimsuit, and draping them over their arm – no bulky basket to slow down their progress. I had my feet trodden on, my ribs jabbed and my fingers jammed between fast-moving hangers. When I picked up a jumper, abandoned by the woman in front of me, she snatched it from my hands.

'That's mine,' she barked, glaring at me as though I'd stolen her wallet.

'You'd put it down,' I said mildly, but she scowled and shoved it in her basket, tutting as though I'd breached some etiquette I knew nothing about.

The following year I hit the sales online instead, and have done so ever since, accepting the lack of rock-bottom prices in exchange for the comfort of my own home.

Sometimes, though, the real bargains are only to be found in person. Last weekend I ventured out into the heart of the Cotswolds, to the sort of home furnishings warehouse sale that over-excites those of us with Aga aspirations but Ikea budgets. From the moment I arrived it was clear you get a better class of bargain-hunter in the Cotswolds. My friend Charlotte − a veteran of such sales − had insisted we be first in the queue, but we were joined very quickly by a pair of Barbour-clad women bearing Waitrose bags for life.

'Well, *they* won't be big enough,' Charlotte whispered gleefully, handing me one of the three enormous laundry bags she'd brought to use as baskets.

'Fill them with whatever you can lay your hands on,' she instructed me. 'You can sort the wheat from the chaff later.'

I was beginning to feel rather alarmed, experiencing Next flashbacks that were making me wonder if I might be suffering from post-traumatic shopping disorder. Yet despite the growing queue, no one was jostling, no one was arguing, and there was little more than a collective tut when someone rocked up five minutes before the gates opened, joining their friends at the front of the now-lengthy queue. This was no Black Friday scrum.

At 10 a.m. exactly, the gates opened and fifty women poured through like refugees from the Boden catalogue. Separated from Charlotte, I found myself swept along, picking up things I never knew I needed. (I'm not entirely sure how I ended up with four cream enamel containers, each with CAKE printed on the side, but at 10 per cent of the retail price, how could I refuse?) Getting into the swing of things, I put my hand on a rather attractive artisan bread bin, just as another woman did the same. Scenes of the Next sale Rottweiler popped into my head, and I backed away.

'Oh, you have it,' the woman said cheerily.

'But it's the last one,' I replied. 'I'm sure you were here first.'

'To be honest,' the woman said chummily, 'there's absolutely nothing wrong with our current bread bin. I'll have to sneak all this lot past my husband as it is. You have it.'

I didn't really want a bread bin, but after such generosity I felt compelled to put it in my bag. The same happened at the next pallet, where a large lady was extolling the virtues of glass storage jars, just a pound each.

'Perfect for marmalade,' she told me, as though we were best friends mid-conversation. 'Or fill them with home-made cookies for end-of-term teacher presents.'

Dutifully, I picked up half a dozen, already feeling the pressure of having to actually make gifts for teachers, instead of thrusting a bottle of wine into their hands with a hastily written thank-you note. Perhaps I could use them as paperweights instead. My bags full, I staggered back out to the yard, where helpful young men were wandering about with calculators.

'How much do you reckon you've got?' one of the chaps said, peering at my haul.

'I'm not altogether sure,' I said. 'I stopped counting at about thirty pounds.'

'Thirty quid it is, then.'

I handed over the notes, cursing myself for not having suggested twenty, and hauled my booty to the car. They say the measure of a bargain is the fact that you'd still have bought it, had it been full price. If that's the case I'm not going to lie: I spent more than I saved. But I now have a spare bread bin, enough cake tins to keep up with the constant PTA demands, something made out of slate that could possibly be a cheese board, and a sign that says 'Gone Sailing', which will be invaluable if we ever buy a boat.

More importantly, my ribs and toes survived unbroken, and you can't put a price on that.

Anti-social media

I am falling out of love with social media. As platforms for observation and communication, they have become essential components of my life as a writer. Alone in my study I can access the inner thoughts of Instagramming celebrities, tweeting Trump followers, and breadline bloggers sharing budget recipes. I can chat to readers on Facebook and find out (with often painful clarity) their literary likes and dislikes, or send a request for niche research to be retweeted a thousand times. Never before has a writer had such wealth of human material at their fingertips; such instant channels of communication. Never before have there been so many writers – for social media has made writers of us all. So why, in this exciting, vibrant world of social media, with its tapestry rich in material and ripe for communication, do I find myself stepping not towards social media but away?

We all have the same time. Eighty years, give or take. Fifty-two weeks a year. Twenty-four hours a day. We can spend those hours where we wish, and too many of mine are disappearing into the void of social media. Time that passes enjoyably slowly while reading a newspaper seems to race past when reading online. I fall down a rabbit hole of Facebook posts, clicking mindlessly from one to the other.

Social media will continue to chip away at our attention spans until we become intolerant of anything delivered in paragraphs; baby birds demanding news in beak-sized bites. There is much skill in the short story format (The infamous 'For sale: baby shoes, never worn' snippet would surely have debuted on Twitter, had it existed), but nothing rivals the emotional arc of a novel.

One of the wonders of social media is discovering one's tribe. Like-minded people with whom one can discuss fashion, sport, or any other subject on earth. But where there is a tribe, there are comparisons; and where there are comparisons, there is disappointment. The baker who shares pictures of her cakes online loses her satisfied glow when she scrolls through other people's creations. The selfie queen proud of her pout wilts a little beside the competition. My own self-esteem takes a hit when someone else's book success hits the social media headlines, even if – five minutes earlier – the offline me was perfectly content with my lot.

We perpetuate this confidence-knocking vortex by posting only the highlights of our lives; the tips of icebergs hiding murky truth beneath the waters. For every Facebook status about my *adorable* children there are ten unwritten updates about arguments, tantrums, dinners untouched and days out ruined. I may write my fictional characters with searing honesty, but I edit my life with social media filters.

I worry we are losing the ability to form our own

opinions; to consider what we *really* think, without the influence of trending hashtags and fake news. Are we morally outraged because our values have been challenged, or because Twitter says we are morally outraged?

Privacy is an oft-raised argument against social media. The regular Facebook 'check-ins' that tell a would-be stalker when we visit the gym; the running app that gives an attacker our route. The airport selfie letting burglars know we'll be away; the photo of our kids with a glimpse of school logo. Snippets of a day, making up a jigsaw of our lives for a stranger's benefit.

Less debated, but just as concerning to me, is the invasion of our emotional privacy. Today's novelists are expected to lay bare their souls, to afford their audiences three-dimensional reading and an access-all-areas pass. Readers don't only want to know what inspired their favourite book, they want to know about the author's family, her pets, her hobbies. They've bought the book – now they want a pound of flesh, too.

Facebook, Twitter, Instagram, internet forums . . . incredible technological advances sparking conversations across the world. Without them, our lives (this writer's life, certainly) would be poorer; our observational well shallower. Yet we would be wise to exercise caution.

There is a life to be found outside social media, and it's better lived unfiltered.

Don't be so grateful

I don't remember when I became a feminist. It might have been when I realised the girls at my high school did home economics instead of Latin, or it might have been when I discovered my grandmother had been required to leave her teaching job once she was married. Either way, by the time I joined the police, fresh out of university, I was what is so frequently (and so disparagingly) referred to as a raging feminist.

'Actually, it's PC,' I'd say politely when someone prefixed my surname with WPC.

My police tutor was aggravated by such 'unnecessary' feminism.

'The "W" makes it easy for control room to despatch female officers if there's a job involving . . .' He searched for an example. 'A lost child,' he finished, triumphantly.

Apparently possessing breasts and a vagina made me a better parental figure than being a father of four.

The police – by the time I joined – did at least offer equal pay and conditions, regardless of one's genitals, and by and large I enjoyed my career without significant discrimination. I accepted that sexism was often a generational issue, forgiving the 'here, let me carry that heavy baton for you' offers that generally came from a chivalrous place, not a sexist one, and I bit my tongue when a town councillor apologised for not offering me a cup of tea because 'the wife isn't here to make it'.

I was a committed feminist, but a quiet one. And then Me Too happened. A dozen allegations of sexual harassment at the hands of men in power became a hundred, became a thousand. Women, finding strength in numbers, shared their #MeToo moments, and encouraged others to do the same.

It was − it is − a revolution.

So obvious and so necessary does equality seem to me, that although I concede that not all men feel the same, I always assumed every woman was − by some sort of genetic default − a feminist.

Who wouldn't want equal pay? Equal status? Who wouldn't want their daughters to be treated fairly? And, once accepting such views, who wouldn't advocate women's rights in order to achieve equality?

Oh, how green I was . . .

At a conference recently, I was in the audience when a successful woman was introduced by the male presenter as 'someone I'd like to snog'. I heard the ripple of unease around me; the exchange of glances. *Did he really just say that?*

I saw the appalled look on the woman's face as she took to the stage, her professional achievements exchanged for her physical attributes in one casually sexist remark. I was shocked and angry enough to complain, and glad when it was taken seriously. A printed apology, an agreement that what was said had been unacceptable. Over and done with.

And yet . . .

There was a backlash. Not from men, but from women.

It was a joke, a bit of fun, a compliment, these women said.

Jealousy, one concluded.

Any woman over fifty should be grateful for the attention, said another.

Grateful? I have never felt *grateful* for attention from anyone.

Not in my twenties, when I was confident and nubile, or in my thirties, when I was tired and stretch-marked. I am not grateful now, in my forties, and I will not be grateful in my fifties. If men are attracted to me I hope it is as much for my brain and my sense of humour as it is for my lips and my legs. If they're not, then I think it's unlikely I'm missing out.

Ladies, have some self-respect. Maybe you don't want to call yourself a feminist. Maybe you think (erroneously) it's impossible to be a feminist without also knitting your own sanitary pads and plaiting your armpit hair (though neither of these would make you a bad person). But do you *really* believe that your contribution to society is less important than a man's?

Newsflash: it isn't.

Ladies, be loud and proud, and don't be ashamed of being a feminist. And never, ever be grateful.

The last supper

Last night at supper we debated a variation of the death-row conundrum: what would you order for dinner if your head was on the block tomorrow? We called our (slightly less macabre) version the 'for ever food' question: what meal would you choose, if you could only ever eat that meal three times a day for ever and ever and ever?

'Steak,' said Josh, who from the age of four knew exactly what he wanted at every restaurant we ever visited, and has never once changed his choice. That boy has expensive tastes (or a lack of imagination).

'Salad,' declared George, whose fondness for lettuce knows no bounds.

Evie struggled to decide. 'Chilli con carne,' she plumped for eventually. 'With tortilla and guacamole and grated cheese. That way, if I get bored, I can just have a cheese wrap. Or an avocado one.' The kid's smart.

Clearly she gets it from me, because my own for ever food strategy follows a similar line of thought. One meal, for ever and ever? Easy. I'd have a picnic.

Oh, how I love a picnic! It is a continual source of disappointment to me that picnic season is considered to run only alongside the summer months, because I would happily snack on pork pies and cocktail sausages at any time of year. Nor do I require a beach or sunny park for my buffet spread: I have eaten picnics in the pouring rain on a cliff top, sitting in a traffic jam on the M1, and – one famous summer – crammed into the boot of my people-carrier, to avoid a particularly vicious wasp invasion.

Not to be reserved for bank holidays, picnics are an any time, any place meal, and one of the few I enjoy making as much as I enjoy eating. Perhaps it's because one doesn't so much cook a picnic as compile it (I suspect someone, somewhere – almost certainly in London – is *curating* one . . .), which makes for the sort of haphazard result that can never, ever be wrong.

In fact, the only thing I *don't* like about a picnic is carrying the bloody thing. Whether it's an Instagrammable wicker basket that lets in the flies, or an insulated cool box that bangs against your legs, transporting one's efforts from kitchen to picnic spot is quite literally a pain in the neck.

Worth it, though, for the spread on arrival. Even the most nondescript sandwiches look better when arranged prettily on a tartan rug, and it's common knowledge that all food tastes better out of doors. Not for me the trendy recipe books with their suggestions of stuffed focaccia and beetroot hummus; I stick to the basics. Hard-boiled eggs and sausage rolls with flaky pastry; ham sandwiches with fiery mustard. Carrot sticks and bowls of cherry tomatoes so we don't get scurvy. Packets of crisps, and chocolate biscuits melting together in the car.

Everything I learned about picnics I learned from my

mother (and Enid Blyton – lashings of ginger beer, anyone?) and now the very act of hauling out the picnic box from the garage is enough to transport me back thirty years. Only now it's *my* children asking if it's time for lunch yet; *my* children taking lids off plastic boxes like they're digging for treasure, then handing me sandwich wrappings and empty yoghurt pots like I'm a human dustbin. It's *my* children eating too much and being sick in the car on the way home.

'What would you have for your for ever meal, Daddy?' Evie asked. *Roast beef*, we guessed. *Salmon? Steak and kidney pie? Curry?* He reached across the table for my hand, and his voice softened.

'I'd share Mummy's picnic, of course.'

The children made sicking noises at this public demonstration of affection, but I didn't care. I squeezed his hand.

'Okay. But you have to carry it.'

Fashion police

Forget coastal rescue, the RNLI and public announcements about sunstroke; the emergency service most needed during a British summer is the fashion police. What is it about the summer season that provokes such sartorial crimes? Men and women who for ten months of the year dress in perfectly normal attire lose their minds at the merest hint of warm weather.

As the first of the spring flowers push their way through warm soil, so Brits push their winter wardrobe to one side. Out with the subdued navy tops, the beige chinos and the tailored skirts. In with the garishly patterned shirts, shapeless shorts and tropical motifs. On a sunny day in Stow-on-the-Wold the pavements are dotted with brightly coloured tourists, their optimistic sun hats at a jaunty angle. The men wear shorts, the cargo pockets stuffed so fat with wallets and phones they have to turn sideways to fit through doors. They show off hairy white legs, almost as shocked by this newfound exposure to daylight as the rest of us are to witness it. Socks with sandals, or – horror of horrors – Crocs.

Above the waist, the picture's no prettier. If you're lucky, you'll find a novelty T-shirt. *My Other Wife's A Supermodel*, or *Is it Beer O'Clock Yet?* Sadly, not every British male is as restrained, and a sunny day could see you staring straight down the barrel of that Englishman-abroad staple: the singlet. Who invented this ghastly piece of clothing? Who on earth thought we might like to be treated to an up close and personal tour of a stranger's armpit hair – not to mention a glimpse of nipple when they lean forward? If ever there was a garment worthy of its own Room 101, it's the singlet.

I'd like to say that women are less likely to commit fashion atrocities, but sadly this is one area of crime that doesn't discriminate between genders. Only last week I encountered a woman in the frozen food aisle with shorts so brief I wanted to drop some talc in her basket to help with the chafing. The summer – such as it is in the UK – seems to herald a silent decree to bare as much flesh as possible. Women whip out their cellulite and wobble crêpey bosoms into strappy vests, despite the temperature rarely getting above 18 degrees Celsius.

'But it's summer!' they cry, teeth chattering above acres of goose-pimpled flesh. Socks are relegated to the back of the drawer, so that we are instead blessed with the sight of cracked heels and athlete's foot; the overall effect made worse, not better, by the last-minute addition of coral nail polish.

How I wish we'd take some tips from other nations when it comes to summer fashion. Take a mooch through a Provençal village on a summer's day and you'll see cool white linens, draped chiffon and broad-brimmed hats. The men wear open-necked cotton shirts; the women flowing skirts and large shades. Not a neon singlet or a pineapple motif in sight.

The problem, of course, is the sun. Or rather, the lack of it. In countries where good weather is guaranteed – when the heat is a nuisance, even – there is no compulsion to strip off. The Tuscan accountant can wait for the weekend to sunbathe on her terrace, and feels no need to wear a strapless mini-dress to the office. Her British equivalent, on the other hand, knows that a day of sunshine is a thing to be cherished. Regardless of the forecast, these glorious few hours could be the last time the sun is spotted this summer. Tomorrow the clouds will return, the rain will fall, and the opportunity to feel heat on bare skin will have been lost.

It is, then (like most things in Britain), the weather's fault that we dress so appallingly in the summer months. And since there is little chance of things improving on that front, there is no alternative but to go with the flow.

Time to dig out those shorts – to hell with the cellulite.

AUGUST

August rain: the best of the summer gone, and the new fall not yet born. The odd uneven time.

Sylvia Plath

The hedgerows are filled with blackberries. So many blackberries. Enough for crumbles and pies, syrups and jams. Enough for the children, whose purple-stained fingers pop two berries in their mouths for each one in the dish.

And enough for you, more selective about what makes your basket. Just the right ripeness, the right juiciness. Not so much that it falls apart in your fingers, or so little that it puckers your mouth with its tartness. You stretch for the brambles at the back, at the top, frustrated by what you can't grasp. Why are the best berries always out of reach? But then you look at what's right in front of you – what *is* in your grasp – and you realise that it is enough. It is more than enough.

At Kineton's Lodge Farm the sunflowers turn their faces upwards, a sea of yellow stretching far as you can see. They are pick-your-own, fifty pence a stem for a local charity, but you would pay four times that for the joy of walking through the field in your big floppy hat, secateurs searching for just the right target. She has told you what to look for, the woman who runs the farm. She has told you not to be fooled by the flowers with soft centres, like the sunflowers from paintings, but to choose the ones where the centre is tight and hard. Those sunflowers will bloom in your kitchen, they will last and last, and when they are finally over you can rub the seeds from the centre, and next year grow your own.

The swifts have gone, headed for South Africa, and leaving the sky empty of their graceful flights. Even the feeders in the garden are empty, as the house sparrows reject your seed for the bounty of the harvest fields. It is too hot to garden, too hot to do anything but walk through the ruins at Minster Lovell to the shade by the River Windrush, and peel off your clothes. Too hot to do anything but dive beneath the surface of the water and come up gasping from the cold.

There is lots of swimming, this month. The banks are tight with tourists who have found this place on TripAdvisor and are, even now, bent over their phones, rating the river for the stunning vistas or its lack of gift shop.

You climb out of the water and dry yourself, and you walk back along the footpath to where your car is parked, even though the sun is still high. Let the visitors have this place today, let them enjoy it. You will come again, next month, when the banks will be bare, and you and the ducks will have the river to yourself.

The Cotswolds aren't going anywhere – and neither are you.

Supermarket sweep

My defection from high-end stores to budget supermarket is complete. It isn't the cheap prices that have lured me away (although I can't deny they're a bonus). It isn't the plethora of German salami, the rustic appeal of pasta sauces displayed on pallets, or the curiously misplaced range of ski wear, walking boots and extendable ladders. Such elements undeniably add colour to my weekly shop, but the primary driver lies at the end of my amble around the aisles.

The best part of a budget supermarket is the checkout.

The cashiers are unfailingly cheerful and never bat an eyelid at the copious bottles of wine that find their way onto the conveyor belt. (I was once accosted by a trolley boy at Waitrose as I clinked my alcohol stash into the boot of the car. 'Having a party?' he wanted to know. I didn't like to confess it was unlikely to last till Thursday.)

The first time I shopped at Aldi I didn't know the form. It's an uneasy feeling, like dining at a posh restaurant with too much cutlery to understand, or knowing whether to shake hands or kiss on both cheeks.

'The other way,' the checkout girl insisted, on my first visit.

I looked at her blankly.

'The trolley needs to go the other way.'

I duly spun my trolley backwards, some instinct telling me this was a well-oiled machine into which it would not do to throw a spanner.

'Ready?' she said.

Ready? Ready for what? I didn't recall the checkout staff at Waitrose ever asking me if I was ready.

In fact, 'Ready?' really doesn't do enough to prepare you. They'd do better to shout 'BRACE! BRACE! BRACE!' in the manner of aircraft emergencies, triggering an adrenalin rush that would at least give you a fighting chance of keeping up with what comes next. Because this is where budget supermarkets and the more salubrious establishments part company.

Once the Aldi (or Lidl – they're cut from the same cloth) checkout operative makes eye contact with you, confirming your readiness, the real action begins. Foodstuffs fly across the scanner at a rate of knots, piling up to the right of the till until you sweep them into your waiting trolley (positioned in the only way that works for such speedy purchasing). It is at once terrifying and exhilarating. No bags are allowed (you'll understand why once you've tried it for yourself – there simply isn't time), and so begins a fast-paced, three-dimensional, middle-aged version of Tetris that I'm not embarrassed to say gives me far more of a buzz than any computer game. Tins of tuna, here; fresh meat, here; cereal packets, pasta and bread here. On and on it comes, faster and faster. Pause to rearrange the fruit and you're lost: food piles up at an alarming rate, leaving you with no alternative but to simply sweep it into your trolley with one all-encompassing arm.

For those of you used to self-scanning your Waitrose Essentials into reinforced green bags, it is perhaps a little basic, but the thrill of correctly slotting each fast-moving item into an appropriately sized space in one's trolley should not be underestimated. From there, you can wheel your trolley to the car park, taking time to decant it into bags and into the boot of your car.

It is this second element that has lured me away from the high street. I am slightly − no, make that extremely − obsessive about the way my weekly shop finds its way into bags. Milk with cheese, meat in one bag, salad items nestled together . . . well-organised shopping bags make unpacking the groceries − surely the worst part − a much more straightforward task.

Nothing makes my heart sink faster in Sainsbury's than the sight of eager Beavers clutching empty plastic bags and rattling a collection tin.

'Here's a quid,' I said, the last time I encountered a colony, 'but it's fine − I'll pack my own bags.'

'But Badger said we need to be helpful,' said the quivering Beaver, picking up a packet of cornflakes.

'Really, it's fine,' I said through gritted teeth, keeping a firm hand on my Kelloggs.

We had a tug-of-war with the cereal for a moment, before Badger herself, a busty, woggle-wearing woman, bore down on us with a face like a bulldog sucking a lemon. Shamed into silence, I watched two eight-year-olds stuff pak choi (salad drawer) and cotton buds (bathroom) into the same bag as fabric conditioner (utility room) and bagels (bread bin – I despair!), and reluctantly surrendered my loose change.

If the bargain prices alone weren't enough to make me take my custom to a budget supermarket, such checkout assaults from juvenile muggers certainly are. When the new branch of Aldi opened in Chipping Norton it was an instant hit with the residents. Apparently the Beavers weren't so keen.

Giving the chickens the chop

The chickens have gone. Between you and me, I'm rather relieved – they were making me terribly fat. A few years ago, back-garden chickens were the preserve of those living in rural idylls, with hundred-foot gardens surrounded by hedgerow. Now everyone I know has chickens, and we're all over-run with eggs. Mums skulk around the school gate like middle-class dealers, pushing half a dozen eggs on anyone who will take them. As the non-chicken-owning market dwindles, so the eggs pile up and it's back home to bake yet more biscuits, even more cake. I was baking every day. The children loved it, but Rob would groan as temptation wafted his way once again, and the scales groaned even louder when I stepped on them. I hid them in a cupboard and baked some more.

We all love the little taste of self-sufficiency, we chicken-keepers, as we position our coops next to our narrow patch of vegetables. It's true the eggs taste better than anything a supermarket can offer, and the morning ritual of egg-collection gives one a warm glow that is hard to replicate elsewhere. When the children were at school and the weather was fine, I would hang the washing on the line and feel the sun on my back as the hens clucked their way around the garden. There is little better to feed the soul, in my book.

It's not all roses, of course, and I weathered the red mite, the lice and the culling. I diligently scrubbed the coop once a week, and jet-washed the chicken yard, and I put up with the temperamental laying that meant either feast or famine.

I drew the line at rats.

I saw one, just as the sun went down, scurrying across the chicken run and out of view. The rat man, who came the next day, said it was part and parcel of having chickens.

'You can get rid of the rats, but they'll come back,' he said.

I considered my options for about a second. The chickens had to go.

He located the probable nest − burrowed deep in the compost bin − and left an unfeasibly large amount of poison in a location he assured me would be too tempting to resist. 'You never get just one rat, you know,' he offered conversationally. 'They breed quickly.' I shuddered.

Half the poison had gone by the morning, and ten days later the rat man proclaimed the issue sorted. His discreetly plain van meant that I had successfully kept our vermin problem quiet from the neighbours, until a few days later, when the children were playing in the garden with friends.

'There's a mouse under the trampoline!' screamed George. I shot outside, darting between the trampoline and the tribe of children, whose excitement surpassed anything seen this side of Christmas morning. 'Look! Look! A mouse! A mouse with a long tail and huge big teeth!'

I intercepted an inquisitive playmate, bent on investigating this furry plaything, and herded everyone to the other side of the garden like a canine contestant in *One Man and His Dog*.

'Just calm down,' I said, not feeling in the slightest bit calm. Where precisely was the rat? What if it wasn't dead? What if it was even now running towards me? I danced around a little bit, to deter it from running up my trouser-leg. 'There's no need to get excited,' I told them, 'it's just a little rat.' I turned round and peered under the trampoline. Blimey, quite a big rat, then.

'A RAT?' Josh bellowed, the sound bouncing neatly into each neighbouring garden. 'An actual rat? A rat in our garden? We've got rats?'

'Don't keep saying it,' I hissed. The rat was definitely dead. Two huge yellow teeth protruded from his open mouth. I grimaced.

'Can we play with it?'

'No.'

A plastic bag was fetched, and the rat deposited gingerly inside, whereupon all the children insisted on taking a proper look.

'Wow,' they sighed, 'a real rat! How exciting!'

Let's hope the neighbours agree.

The second pony

A friend of a friend is in dire straits. I know this because I have seen her status update shared several times on Facebook by mutual acquaintances.

'Urgent!' the appeal reads. 'We are desperately searching for a second pony for Tabitha.'

Gosh.

Desperately searching.

Not just looking. Not idly thinking that perhaps it might be nice to have one, but *desperately* searching. All that angst, all those sleepless nights! My heart bleeds. Whatever will they do? Even ignoring the desperation, let's just consider the fact that this search is for a *second* pony: darling Tabitha has already had one, which frankly is one more than about 99 per cent of the population. What was wrong with the first one? Is it on some kind of flexible working pattern? Compressed hours? Does it refuse to work on the Sabbath? Is Tabitha jettisoning her first pony, or planning to ride them in tandem, like a circus performer?

I can't help but feel Tabitha's parents have lost their sense of perspective. Unless pony number two is blessed with life-giving properties, knows next week's lottery numbers, or can do the school run, make macaroni cheese and fold the laundry, I really don't think *desperate* is the word I'd use (and if you do happen to hear of such a wonder-horse, never mind Tabitha – you knew me first . . .).

I darkly suspect that, if I knew Tabitha's mother, I would also find her to be *desperate* for kitchen suppers, a Denby dinner service, and several Boden skirts sporting 'witty' designs. That's assuming she doesn't have them already. The Cotswold status-symbol catalogue clearly now includes pets.

There's no doubt about it: you get a certain breed of pet-owner in the Cotswolds. There must be more spaniels per square mile than anywhere else in the country, almost all owned by people who – let's be honest – secretly wish they had horses as well (you can tell by the pseudo-jodhpurs and the quantity of tweed). Those lucky enough to own horses don't ride any old nag: they have steeds with names that take up two lines in the Pony Club newsletter, shiver if they spend too long outside, and feast on organic oats from a gold-plated trough.

Cotswold ponies are sleek and well bred, stabled overnight and sold on after two years in favour of something bigger and better. Impossible to think of one horse doing everything, of course – as poor Tabitha has clearly found: there's the polo pony, the showjumper, the eventer, the dressage horse, the general hack . . . It's exhausting just thinking about it.

I've got nothing against equestrians; I rode as a child, but on a grass-fed Thelwell lookalike who hurled me over (and occasionally through) two-foot fences with grass sticking out of his mouth, and eyes that looked in different directions. I bounced happily on top with my hat askew, my shirt untucked, and a red rosette for ever out of my grasp. There was nothing sleek about either of us.

Our family horses (yes, yes, we did have two, but there *were* three of us) were hardy Welsh mountain and New Forest ponies on long-term loan from another family, and they stayed with us until we went off to university. Blessed with a slender figure into my late teens (those were the days . . .), I carried on riding little thirteen-hand Ricky until my feet were barely inches off the ground. It made leaping on and off during gymkhana races a doddle, but I got terribly wet at the water jump. Both ponies were used to rattling along a road barefoot, turning their noses up at the idea of expensive shoes. They were happy in their muddy field all year round, needing nothing more than a slice of hay and a handful of pony nuts if the snow was making it tricky to find the grass. Both ponies were blissfully low-maintenance, but even low-maintenance horses cost an arm and a leg in vet's bills and insurance. Not to mention those things you use to get stones out of their feet.

Twenty years on money is tight and horses – even low-maintenance ones – are out of the question for me and my tribe. If the children want to learn to ride they'll have to use their imagination: slap a saddle on the spaniel and call it Silver.

Maybe Tabitha's parents should do the same. It'd be a darn sight cheaper – and, after all, they are *desperate*.

Wish you were here

Ah, holidays BC (Before Children). Remember those? Faliraki foam parties, booze cruises to Calais, sun-baked Spanish beaches . . . It was another life entirely, back when you could see your feet without leaning forward, and before walking upstairs sounded like someone had strapped crisp packets to your knees.

In the first few years after meeting Rob we would take off to sunnier shores each summer. Him, me, a map of France and a tent just big enough for a blow-up mattress and a battery-powered radio. His Citroën Saxo (it was that or my MG Midget, and its tendency to discard pieces of metal at inopportune moments) had no air conditioning, and in traffic we'd hang out of the rolled-down windows like panting dogs, desperate to pick up speed just so we could cool down. We'd take turns to take the wheel, non-stop down to La Rochelle, one of us always waking with a start in the early hours to find the other was driving on the wrong side of the road in a (fortuitously) deserted street. When we were too knackered to drive any more we'd pitch our tent at the first campsite we found, drinking cheap wine and having noisy sex before emerging at noon the following day, forced out by sun on canvas.

They were heady, happy days.

When we have kids, we said, *we'll still do this*. Road trips, camping holidays, round-the-world backpacking. We would fly to foreign climes, explore exotic cultures, taste every food going. Our children would be worldly wise and full of adventure. No package deals for us, no kids' clubs or entertainers or all-inclusive ice-cream buffets.

Oh, how little we knew about life After Children . . .

With three under fifteen months, and five hundred nappies a month at their peak, it was a while before holidays featured in our budget at all. An invitation to join the in-laws in Portugal was incredibly generous, but all I remember from the week is breastfeeding twins in the cool of the villa while everyone else swam in the sun, and the sound of three children screaming for the three-hour flight there and back again.

Never again, we said.

Kids don't need to go abroad anyway, we said.

We tried a hotel, once, on a short break to London, not realising we'd be trapped in our room from 7 p.m., drinking warm wine out of plastic toothmugs and speaking in whispers because the babies were finally asleep.

'We could take it in turns to go and have a drink in the bar,' I suggested.

It wasn't quite the holiday atmosphere we'd hoped for.

Self-catering cottages were the answer, and remained the answer for several years. Wales, Devon, Scotland . . . Sometimes in the sun, mostly in the rain, always having a fun, if exhausting, time.

'I need another holiday now,' was the usual refrain on

our return, self-catering holidays being really quite hard work. They require, of course, the usual chores – shopping, cooking, washing up – but without any of one's usual home comforts (assuming you consider a washing machine, DVD player plus a variety of Disney films, and a bed that's actually wide enough for two people who aren't hobbits to be home comforts).

A few years on, and we were ready to try a Proper Holiday. I yearned for reliable sunshine and warm water; fat tomatoes and salty feta; rosé drunk indecently early.

The first few websites brought me up with a jolt. How much? For a holiday? Enticing bargains early in the calendar gave way to eye-watering prices once you started looking at August.

Could I take the children out of school? Aged nine, I was poorly at home the day my class did long division, and to this day I can't split a restaurant bill without a calculator. What might my children miss in a whole week of lessons?

I gazed at a photo of an azure sea, laughing families frolicking in the surf.

Mind you, who doesn't have a calculator on their phone nowadays? And don't they say that family holidays can be just as educational as school?

We booked the next day.

It was perfect. Just perfect. The children are old enough to stay up as late as us. They're old enough to spend a plane journey immersed in a book, a film, or some unintelligible game. They're old enough to have interesting conversations, to argue their viewpoint and celebrate victory or concede defeat with (mostly) good grace. They load the dishwasher and make their beds. They love restaurants as much as we do. They will play in the pool for an entire day, while I supervise from a sun-lounger, slipping into the water only when it gets too hot.

I can read books again!

We have reached Optimum Family Holiday Age.

By my calculations we have approximately five summers left before my happy, biddable children morph into glooming, monosyllabic teens who sleep till sundown, think Greece is *lame* and mutter constantly *Why couldn't I have gone to Magaluf like everyone else?*

I'd better book another holiday.

WI revellers

I wanted to join the Women's Institute for years. There is something remarkable about what women can achieve when they get together, and the WI's campaign record is impressive to say the least. Besides, I make a mean Victoria sponge and I'd always wanted to try my hand at quilting.

When I moved to the Cotswolds I made enquiries about joining my local WI. It was a charming group with twenty or so elderly ladies who made superb cakes and had no end of advice and stories to tell. But – oh, how can I put this? – it just wasn't terribly *me*. The talks didn't inspire me, and meetings were held at lunchtime – tricky for anyone with a job or with young children.

Undaunted, I approached head office and was bowled over by their enthusiasm for my tentative suggestion that we form a second WI in Chipping Norton, with meetings to be held in the evenings.

Needless to say, the birth of a brand-new WI alongside an existing one was not without its issues. Opening the door one day I was met by two pensioners, beady eyes black with resentment.

'There isn't room for two WIs,' one of them said. Was this the modern-day equivalent of *This town ain't big enough for the both of us?* What happens instead of a shoot-out? Twenty paces, then turn and show off your jam? The turf war had begun, and it wasn't pretty.

I took to avoiding the farmers' market for fear of being pelted with fruit cake.

A few weeks after our launch, as I was out walking with the children, a lady in her seventies approached me.

'Are you the girl responsible for setting up a new WI?' she asked.

I braced myself, nodding nervously.

The woman glanced around and whispered furtively, 'Is there room for any more? It sounds terribly fun.'

Fun it certainly has been, with the wine-tasting session a particular highlight. The 'Oxford butler' coped admirably with the heckling from a roomful of middle-aged mothers and tactfully managed our uneducated questions about the best three-for-two offers at Waitrose. Just as we were swirling around the contents of our first glass, a dark-haired woman pushed open the door and asked whether she was in the right place for the church meeting.

'Upstairs,' we chorused, well-versed now in directing people around the parish rooms.

She hesitated, her hand on the door. 'So what meeting is this?'

'We're West Oxfordshire WI,' our president announced proudly. 'We're wine-tasting.'

With some reluctance, the visitor bade us farewell and headed upstairs to her meeting.

Half an hour later we were on to our third wine and happily discussing our new-found expertise when the door creaked open again. The dark-haired woman smiled broadly, dropped her money into the pot and picked up a glass. 'There's a lot to be said for getting lost,' she said.

I suspect (although the vicar may disagree) that she made the right decision. By the end of the evening I had learned the following:

The slower the 'legs' running down the inside of the wine glass, the greater the alcohol content.

Almost every red wine benefits from being given time to breathe.

The pub is an excellent place to continue practising one's wine-tasting skills after hours.

Despite it being more than a decade since I last tried, I can still put my leg behind my head.

And do a cartwheel.

Going to bed three hours before the school run is inadvisable.

And finally: hangovers last significantly longer than they did in my twenties.

A pane in the glass

The good weather means I can't ignore it any longer: the windows are in dire need of a clean. Sun streams valiantly through the kitchen window, despite the crust of bird poo and a suspicious layer of green slime.

I shall have to call the window cleaners.

We're not short of good ones, round our way. I see them daily, in their branded polo shirts, zipping around town with ladders on car roofs and boots full of buckets.

I know (because they remind me every time) that it would be more cost-effective to go on their books for a regular clean than to call them up on an ad hoc basis, but I have a deep-seated fear of tradespeople who start work unannounced. I've never quite recovered from emerging from the bathroom in the altogether, only to see the top of a ladder appear at my bedroom window. With nowhere else to go I was forced to dive behind the bed, pressing my naked body into the carpet until it was safe to reappear. It makes for a most disquieting start to the day.

Even when fully clothed it's rather alarming to suddenly see a chap peering into your house. I'm never quite sure what to do: surely it's not good manners to ignore them. Does one wave? Mouth 'hello'? And if one wanders through the house and sees them at several windows in turn, is it correct to acknowledge them on each occasion? Privacy matters aside, it's an interruption I don't welcome. I have the sort of intrinsic work ethic that makes it impossible for me to sit down, flick through a magazine, or watch the latest scintillating episode of *Come Dine With Me* while other people are working. Even if I've nailed my word count for the day and am celebrating with a cup of tea and a Bourbon (the biscuit, not the liquor, although that's not a bad idea . . .), when the window cleaner appears I feel guilt of Catholic proportions, propelling me out of my chair towards whatever housework I can lay my hands on. I once washed up something already clean and on the draining board, just to prove to the window cleaner that I wasn't some lady of leisure. It's all far too stressful.

Last summer I washed the windows myself. Lacking a long-enough ladder, I cleaned the upstairs ones by clutching the windowsill with one hand and leaning precariously out with my sponge. The neighbour opposite sat in the sun and watched me, helpfully informing me only after I'd finished about the 'easy-clean' button that turns the windows inside out to facilitate such a task. Even armed with this knowledge, it's an arduous job, leaving me with windows that – while clean – are so streaked they could pass as frosted. It's a job for the professionals, to be booked for a specific day, when I can brace myself for their arrival and line up some honest toil to do at the same time.

A revealing conversation during drinks with the girls on Friday night suggests I might have been missing out on more than consistently clean windows.

'I visited a friend on the Leys this morning,' Anna told us, referring to a street on the other side of town. 'Goodness, how I wish I lived *there*!' It seems the window cleaner responsible for that particular round has attributes far beyond a squeaky-clean pane of glass.

'Taut biceps,' she elaborated, 'tattoos, a rather lovely beard, and a stomach you could bounce peas off.'

There was a collective pause as six middle-aged women pictured such a stomach, and thought about moving to the Leys.

'Imagine *that* knocking on your door, offering you a go with his squeegee,' one of them said wistfully. Another pause. Somebody sighed.

'Do we know him?' I said.

By 'we', I meant the vast school-gate collective, its tentacles extending across cubs, swimming lessons, cricket club, rugby training . . . We pooled our knowledge, but couldn't put a name to him. There should be some sort of database, we decided. Like Tinder, but for window cleaners. Winder. Housewives everywhere (and indeed house husbands, should they be so inclined – far be it from me to discriminate) could log on and match profiles to rounds. It could be exactly what the property market needs, giving a surprise boost to areas serviced by attractive window cleaners.

In the meantime, however, my own window situation is critical, and in the absence of such a database I shall have to take my chances on the eye-candy front.

What a pane in the glass.

SEPTEMBER

September: it was the most beautiful of words, he'd always felt, evoking orange-flowers, swallows, and regret.

Alexander Theroux

The colours change so swiftly. One minute the trees are lush and verdant, the next they are canopies of reds and golds, pinks and oranges. Soon the colours will fall, until they carpet the ground, and so now is the time for walks in the park, for final picnics in the last of the sun. Now is the time to visit the arboretum at Batsford, to stand beneath trees flaming yellow and crimson, like fireworks lit only for you.

The starlings are growing busy. You see one on his own, first; then two, side by side. A small group on a telegraph wire. And then – oh! – a murmuration. You're in the car, somewhere between Burford and Lechlade, and you pull over, mesmerised by this cloud of dark flecks that sweeps from side to side, swelling to a dense ball in the sky, then stretching to each side, like someone has taken each end and pulled it thin. On and on they dance, never missing a step, never falling out of line. You don't know if you've been watching for five minutes or an hour; you only know that no film, no stage show could ever hold your gaze with such attention as these starlings.

There is a freshness in everything around you – in the new academic year, and the children who walk to school in shirts still creased from the packet – and you can't help but catch some of this eagerness for life. You plant two hundred bulbs in the borders and, like secrets, in the grass around each fruit tree. You harvest what seems like a thousand runner beans, painstakingly stripping the stringy edges from each one. You plunge them first into boiling water, and then into ice, freezing the bags so that – come winter – you will be able to serve home-grown veg with your roasts. You lift the last of the potatoes and spread them out to dry, before placing them carefully in hessian sacks to be stored somewhere dark and cool.

You still make salads, but they are heartier now, with roasted beetroot and cubes of sweet squash; kale and broccoli and crumbled blue cheese. On the first properly cold day you make soup, and remember how comforting it is, and – most importantly – how quick and easy it is, and so you make it most days for the rest of the autumn. While others bemoan the end of barbecues and summer pot lucks, you hanker for shepherd's pies and beef stews.

You have loved the freedom of bare legs and summer linens, but you greet your autumn wardrobe like the return of a friend, slipping into jeans and soft sweatshirts and pushing your sandals to the back of the cupboard.

Each season has something new to offer – something exciting, something different – and you think (as, in fact, you think every season) that this one is your favourite.

Back to school

Autumn has always been my favourite time of year, ever since my own schooldays when the end of summer went hand in hand with a shopping trip for new pens, books and school shoes. With an entire academic year ahead of me, anything felt possible; resolutions as easily made (and broken) now as in January. Even when I left university and the calendar no longer ran from September to July, the autumn continued to feel like the start of the year. Each time I fell pregnant my bump grew as the leaves were falling, and so those autumns, too, were filled with list-making and shopping in preparation for the new arrivals.

And now suddenly my first child is starting secondary school, and I feel just as caught out as I was when he started primary. *I'm not ready for this*, I remember thinking as I ironed his little uniform and cut the crusts off his sandwiches. *I'm not ready to call a teacher by anything other than their first name. I'm not ready to join a PTA, to bake cakes for the summer fête or to stand at the school gate with a bunch of mothers I hope might one day be my friends. I'm not ready to dress up my baby in dark grey trousers and a jumper he'll grow into. And I'm not ready to see him wave to me as he disappears into years I'll never know as intimately as his first five. I'm just not ready.*

I'm not ready now.

Josh, of course, is more than ready. He's excited about this move to high school, about lessons that move from room to room. Excited about taking lunch money, and walking home alone, and having a locker with a key we both know he'll lose by half term. He's moving on.

'I'll take you to WH Smith to buy everything you need for school,' I said.

'We can just get it online,' said Josh, product of the internet age.

I was insistent. 'We have to go to Smith's, it's tradition.' I dragged him to town and we chose a new pencil case, and new pens, and a shatterproof ruler exactly like the one I had at his age. We bought a bag twice the size of him; and a geometry set, the purpose of which has always been a mystery to me.

With only one more year to go at primary school, Evie and George now walk to school on their own, and so on the first day of term I wave all three children down the drive, and I stand alone in the hall, suddenly redundant. I should be cheering, I suppose. Rejoicing in my freedom after six weeks of holidays, and phoning round my friends to arrange celebratory cups of tea.

But here's the thing: I love the summer holidays.

When I gave up work and looked after the children full time, the prospect of the holidays filled me with dread. I approached that first year with military precision, drawing up a daunting spreadsheet of events cross-referenced against

Rob's shifts and colour-coded to ensure an even spread of activity type.

We would bake and craft on alternate days; tour the region's museums; join the National Trust; learn new skills; catch up with friends; and spend hours outdoors. There would be no television, no lethargy, no arguments and above all *no boredom*. I would be serene, imaginative, nurturing and not the slightest bit shouty.

Despite these solemn vows the end of term loomed large on the calendar and I began having nightmares, waking up at three in the morning crying 'Is everyone having fun?'

As it turned out, it was just fine. The days raced by in a blur of play dates, chores and lolling about the house. I revelled in the lazy mornings, letting the children giggle in their pyjamas till noon. We tore up the spreadsheet and went with the flow, and it wasn't nearly as bad as I'd imagined. There were arguments – lots of them – and I did my fair share of shouting. And so there *was* television after all, and that made everything all right.

Ever since then I have embraced the holidays and mourned their passing, with its return to structure and rules and aren't-you-out-of-bed-yets? I don't want to wake up a child that needs to sleep, and I don't want to enforce homework time when the garden is so much more inviting. I don't want to find the stain-remover for a white shirt, or polish shoes, or clean rugby boots. It's all such a lot of *work*.

Oh, but the house is so quiet . . .

The house is quiet, and the kettle is on, and it's just

possible there are still a few biscuits the children haven't scavenged. Because *goodness* they eat a lot when they're home all day, and I've given up tidying when it just ends up messy again.

In fact, I think, as I sink into the sofa with a cuppa and a Garibaldi, maybe the reason I like the holidays so much is that they don't last for ever.

Homework

Secondary school is a whole new ball game. After years of talking to teachers at the primary-school gate, and popping into class to deliver a forgotten PE kit or help out with some reading, the disconnect between secondary school and home takes some getting used to.

'What's your French teacher called?' I ask Josh at the end of week one.

'Dunno.'

'What are you doing in maths?'

'Um, something to do with angles?'

There was a time when I'd grab Mrs Smith and find out myself; there was a time when a letter home would have told me exactly what angles they were looking at this term, and why. But at secondary school the pupils are young adults, encouraged to remember things – and make mistakes – without their parents' intervention.

It's quite a shock to the system, although not an entirely unwelcome one. I can't deny I'm delighted to see the end of reading records, and of dress-up days that required me to produce a Roman soldier outfit with an evening's notice. I don't mourn the model-making, or the parents' race, and I certainly don't mourn Billy the bloody Bear.

During the week, Billy Bear lived – and presumably still does – in reception class, spending each weekend with a different family. Taking Billy home was an honour bestowed on those who listened to the teacher, played nicely and put the toys away when the lunch bell rang. My own children had been waiting all term for Billy to grace them with his presence, and it was amid great excitement that a delighted Josh bounded out of the classroom one Friday with Billy clasped firmly in his arms.

'Look, Mummy! We have to take him *everywhere* with us, and then we have to write about it in his diary!'

I stifled my sighs – not only did I have three children to amuse all weekend, I had to entertain a stuffed bear to boot. Needless to say, despite the initial enthusiasm for the class bear, Billy was swiftly forgotten.

It wasn't until Sunday night, as the children were tucked up in bed and I was halfway through a glass of Sauvignon Blanc, that I caught sight of a pair of glassy eyes staring balefully at me from the mound of toys in the playroom. Bugger.

I located Billy's journal at the bottom of Josh's book bag and gazed wide-eyed at his exploits. Billy was one well-travelled bear. A weekend in Fowey at the annual regatta, a trip to the polo at Cirencester and a Daylesford cookery class were just some of the ways in which he had spent his days.

I mentally scrolled through our own weekend itinerary. Takeaway pizza, too much television and a trip to the dump to get rid of a mattress with dubious stains. Hardly befitting the international playbear described within the pages of his diary. How could I admit to a weekend so devoid of cultural activities, when Billy's diary was positively heaving with trips to the Ashmolean, the Natural History Museum and Tate Modern?

As term progressed, and the parents had become more competitive, so Billy's activities had become more outlandish, more unusual, more exclusive. Some of these later entries were accompanied by supporting evidence in the form of photographs. Here Billy Bear stood tall in fishing waders, holding an enormous pike. Here Billy Bear was scarcely visible beneath his fencing mask, furry legs apart and arm raised in the *en garde* position. And there was Billy Bear sporting ballet shoes as he pirouetted across a floodlit stage.

There was no way we could ever compete.

I polished off the dregs of my wine and sat the bear next to the empty bottle, where he lolled drunkenly to one side. Taking a picture, I printed it out and stuck it in the diary.

Billy might not have done much over the weekend, but he certainly looked as though he enjoyed it.

Twist of fête

I remember vividly the look on my mother's face whenever I came home from school with an envelope full of raffle tickets.

'Ten books?' she'd lament, and then she'd put them on the windowsill with the rest of the household detritus. They would sit there for a month, and on the day the stubs were due back my mother would dutifully write her name on each one and send me to school with an envelope of stubs and money.

Could she not even try *to sell some?* I thought, disappointed by my mother's lack of exertion. Buying them herself may well raise the same amount of money, but where was the effort? Where was the commitment?

I see now that she must have been as worn down by fundraising activities as I am. Sorry, Mummy.

My children had scarcely been at primary school for five minutes before the fundraising appeals began. Could you make a cake? Man a stall? Sponsor a walk? On and on and on it goes, until half term becomes less about a break from the school run and more about a welcome respite from PTA appeals. My three children are so close in age that they will move through school together, limiting my involvement to a mere eight years. For my friends with larger age gaps between children, the fundraising demands are relentless: fifteen-odd years of dishing out tenners like they've been plucked from trees. To add insult to injury, school fundraisers have a knack of making you pay twice: you buy ingredients to make a cake, then you go to the coffee morning and buy another cake.

In common with most voluntary groups, it is the same dozen or so people who do everything. They turn up with increasingly weary smiles after baking till midnight to flog home-made fudge and Christmas cards all day, in order to secure £87.50 for the PTA coffers at an hourly rate that would have trade unions demanding strike action. I have a grudging respect for the parents who brush off the requests for donations; who throw away the newsletter with the frantic appeal for help instead of pinning it to the kitchen noticeboard, from where it issues a daily injection of guilt. If asked directly, these parents say they're too busy, with a patronising look that says 'I have a proper job, in an office, so sadly I'll have to leave the cake-baking to you stay-at-homers.' The irony is that the women – because I'm afraid it is mostly women – who do the most for the PTA are generally the busiest. Nappies to change; businesses to build; charities to run . . . the old adage, if you want something done, ask a busy person, has never been truer.

Ahead of school fête season, local businesses take to hastily putting up closed signs in their windows at the sight of a Boden-clad woman bearing down on them with a clipboard. One school started so early on the quest for raffle prizes this year they had cleaned up before the rest of us were off the starting block. Members of rival PTAs become increasingly tight-lipped about their fête plans, in case another school should swipe their brilliant idea of running a Pimm's tent, live-streaming the snail race or auctioning Mr Smedley. Near-identical posters (clip-art bunting, sunflowers, exclamation marks) pepper every telegraph pole and noticeboard, and every inch of freezer space in the Cotswolds is given over to home-made scones.

When the last lot of raffle tickets came home from our school, I didn't even try to sell them. Everyone in my circle of friends was either attempting to sell their own raffle tickets, or sick of being plagued for money by the myriad PTAs vying for business in the area. I left the tickets on the windowsill for a month, then resolutely filled out each stub with my own name and number, and sent them back to the school office.

'Aren't you even going to try and sell some?' asked Evie, clearly let down by my apparent apathy.

'No, darling,' I said. 'I'm not. And when *you* have children, neither will you.'

Happy hens

Give me a funeral over a hen party any day. The food is far better, the wine as plentiful (although generally lacking such niceties as Jägerbombs and tequila slammers), and no one expects you to dress up in ridiculous clothes. So when the invitation to a hen weekend arrived from a good friend, I have to confess that my heart sank a little.

Between you and me, I didn't even enjoy my own hen party very much. There were certain elements that were fun (wine-tasting, paint-balling, bumping into the entire Bath rugby team on a night out) but there were quite a few that weren't. Staying in a YHA dormitory was not quite the luxury I had envisaged when I passed control of my premarital festivities to a group of friends. Did they not know me *at all*?

The worst part was undoubtedly the dressing up. The obligatory L-plates, the veil, the fluffy wings . . . It still makes me cringe, all these years later. The problem with fancy dress is that however jolly you look en masse, there will come a point at which you have to leave your friends and strike out alone. There is nothing more pathetic than a slightly drunk angel with a lopsided halo, trying to order a Bacardi and Coke. Even if you stick resolutely to your fellow hens, wearing a 'fun' costume means you have to plaster a suitably happy smile on your face AT ALL TIMES. Because you can bet your bottom dollar that the one time you yawn, roll your eyes, look at your watch or narrow your eyes at the bride-to-be you'll be snapped by whichever irritating woman has been nominated as photographer.

Yes, irritating. Unless you're the hen herself, in which case you presumably like everyone there, it is very probable that half of the women will be complete strangers to each other, and at least one of them is bound to irritate the hell out of you.

It was therefore with some trepidation that I accepted my friend Sarah's hen-party invitation. In fact, the only reason I said yes was because she had written at the bottom: 'I'll understand if it's not your thing.' The implication being, 'Look, I know you're at least a decade older than me and my fun-loving chums, so if you'd rather stay at home with a mug of Bovril and *Gardeners' Question Time*, that's okay by me.'

Well, obviously I couldn't let that one go.

'Count me in!' I replied, paying up before I could change my mind.

My reluctance was only partly down to my horror of hen parties, and partly to do with the chosen location.

Sarah planned to celebrate the end of her single days at a *festival*.

A nice, middle-class sort of festival, but nevertheless a festival. I don't do festivals. Even when I was eighteen the thought of queuing in thigh-high mud to use an overflowing loo, while some band I had never heard of played on a stage I could barely see, simply wasn't appealing. The prospect is no more attractive now. So it was with a heavy heart that I packed the car with festival essentials (ear plugs, a goose-down pillow and a good book – what do you mean, that's not what people take to festivals?) and set off to collect three other hens I had never met before.

Within the first half-hour of the journey we had covered sex lives, birth stories, job woes and personal tragedies, and were chatting nineteen to the dozen. Even the heavy traffic didn't dent our spirits, and as we arrived at the festival site I felt a flash of something vaguely familiar.

Was I actually *looking forward* to the weekend?

We passed through security and I heaved my bag onto the table. The security officer paused at a zipped pocket.

'Do you have anything in there you shouldn't have?' he asked. I felt that sudden clutch of fear one always experiences when faced with authority.

'It's my husband's sports bag,' I said. 'I don't know what's in that pocket.'

'I can smell something,' the security man said.

What on earth was in there? Had someone set me up? Was I a . . . was I a MULE?

I swallowed hard as the man unzipped the pocket and pulled out an ancient tube of Deep Heat. I think we were both relieved. Safely inside the festival ground I began to relax. Sarah's friends were warm, funny and welcoming, just like her, and before I knew it I had donned a novelty chicken mask and was simulating sex with a blow-up doll wearing the face of her future husband. I'm so very sorry, James.

The weekend passed in a haze of sunshine, gin-in-a-tin, music and laughter, and although I confess to sneaking off early at bedtime with my book, I had the most fun I've had in ages. Far from blocked Portaloos and burnt burgers, my first festival experience included hot showers and picnics of lentil salad and home-made guacamole. On the last night we were approached by a smart young chap in a straw hat. He asked if we were enjoying ourselves (we were), whether we'd been here before (we hadn't), and whether we needed any pills. We looked at each other.

'Um, I think we're all right, actually,' I said.

He chatted for a while about the various illicit products on offer, prompting the woman next to me to remark upon what a good salesman he was.

'I used to work for John Lewis,' he explained, before bidding us a pleasant evening and wandering off. There was a pause before one of the girls spoke.

'They do train their staff awfully well,' she said. There was a quiet murmur of agreement.

What a jolly nice weekend.

Pets on parade

Why do people dress up their pets? I don't mean blankets for thoroughbred horses, or even coats for whippets (although I can't help but feel they look a little ridiculous. 'Get a proper dog,' I always want to say. 'One with fur'). No, I'm talking about animals wearing actual clothes. Cats in Little Red Riding Hood costumes, dogs dressed as Batman, rabbits in sailor hats. If you don't believe me, google them – they're all there. In every photo the owners are sporting clinically insane smiles (and – occasionally – matching costumes), while the pets' expressions range from mildly bemused to pretty pissed off.

I don't blame them.

What self-respecting boxer wants to wear a tutu? Besides, the day my pets earn the right to flick covetously through the latest White Stuff catalogue is the day they start contributing to the household income. Right now, if there's any spare cash to be spent on fashion, it will be invested in my own wardrobe, not that of my furry friend.

I'm always delighted to be given more excuses to buy clothes (truthfully, I only tried my hand at golf for the nice-coloured polo shirts), and the acquisition of a dog has provided such opportunities in spades. After Maddie arrived I spent a few weeks doing research, eyeing up fellow dog-walkers and jotting down my findings in a little notebook, before heading out to buy the perfect dog-owning outfit. Wellies, naturally (in a colour and pattern combination described incomprehensibly on the website as 'entertaining'), a waxed jacket (ankle-length, to guarantee not only a dry bottom, but also the concealment of pyjama bottoms when I haven't bothered to get dressed before the school run), and a wide-brimmed hat to stop my mascara running in the rain.

The shopping possibilities are endless. I haven't had this much fun since I took up riding and got to buy skin-tight jodhpurs, knee-length boots and quilted gilets (to be worn with the collars permanently turned up). As a criterion for which pet to choose, it's as good as any other. Sure, consider the vet bills, the walks, the way it'll get on with the children, but above anything else, consider how it will impact on your wardrobe.

You could buy the kids a guinea pig, but what good will that be? Despite extensive googling I have struggled to find any outfits suitable for guinea pig owners. Buy a falcon, however, and you get to buy cool leather gloves. It's a win–win situation.

In my efforts to find sartorial options for other small-animal lovers I have come across a book – now sadly out of print – called *Knitting with Dog Hair*. The tagline to this handy manual (as if you needed any more encouragement) reads 'Better a sweater from a dog you know and love than from a sheep you'll never meet.'

Well, quite. Although given the amount of fox poo that

finds its way into Maddie's coat, I'm not certain I'd be welcomed with open arms at the next WI meeting if I was wearing a creation made from her discarded hair.

Still, if you're keen to wear your Persian's fur somewhere other than on the seat of your suit trousers, you'll be relieved to know that the content of *Knitting with Dog Hair* is far wider than the title suggests. You can make an Afghan from an Afghan hound, turn Tabby into trousers and recycle your rabbit. Just steer clear of anyone with allergies.

Horsing around

As we grow closer to a moving date, Evie is distraught. The new house is too far from the stables to carry on riding. The last year has seen her taking to the saddle like the proverbial duck to water, with a natural seat and an affinity with her steed that I'm not sure I ever had, but her blossoming hobby is coming to a halt as abruptly as a refusal at Becher's Brook.

Long-promised gymnastics have provided a useful distraction, but neither of us – I suspect I will miss our weekly dose of stable life at least as much as her, if not more – is quite ready to give up on riding. I thought perhaps the answer was to be self-sufficient. A pony of our own. Something small at first, and then an upgrade to something big enough for Evie and me to share the exercising load. I thought back to the halcyon days of my Pony Club childhood, and imagined how wonderful it would be to look out of the kitchen window and see a horse in the field beyond the garden.

A glance at the *Horse & Hound* message board, however, prompted a fall at the first. As children we kept our horses in a farmer's field, paying peppercorn rent in exchange for accepting the more-wire-than-post fencing, the lack of proper stables, and a muck-heap that was less banked and more dumped. We rode tubby, hardy ponies who turned their noses up at shoes, ate nothing but grass and the occasional slice of winter hay, and bounded happily over a motley collection of straw bales and broom handles. There was, of course, a cost (not least to my mother, who in the winter valiantly drove to the field each morning before school to break the ice on the water trough), but it was manageable.

Nowadays it seems impossible to keep a horse without shelling out as much each month as one's mortgage payment. Ongoing field management, six-weekly farrier visits, insurance, dental checks, inoculations, tack, rugs, feed, vet fees, bedding, worming . . . I could put one of the children through private school for the same money, without the need to check for ragwort.

'I'm sorry,' I tell Evie on our way to gymnastics, 'we just can't afford it.'

I don't add that, even if we did have the money, the additional knowledge gleaned from my *Horse & Hound* research means that the prospect of keeping horses now fills me with fear. Moving from casual pony ownership to well-informed horse husbandry weighs heavy not only on the pocket, but on one's paranoia. There's so much to go wrong that it seems a miracle my childhood ponies survived to complete as many clear rounds as they did, given our family's reliance on common sense, an ancient copy of *Keeping a Pony at Grass* and a trusted friend who knew slightly more about horses than we did.

At my declaration Evie's bottom lip quivers. I head off

the tears and chivvy her out of the car towards the gymnastics hall.

'Anyway,' I say brightly, pointing at the equipment laid out in the hall. 'You've got a horse here.'

Evie gives me a withering look worthy of a woman my own age. I contemplate asking her why the long face, but decide against it. There's only so much horsing around a mother can get away with.

OCTOBER

October's foliage yellows with his cold.

John Ruskin

In a fortnight, the fields have turned from gold to brown, deep furrows ploughed up and down each one. When you walk along the edges your boots gather clumps of mud until your feet are too heavy to lift, and you have to lean against a gate and scrape the soles with a stick. You catch the movement of a mouse, scurrying into the hedgerow, but otherwise the fields are still. You wish you knew about mushrooms – had confidence in their similarities to the pictures in books – because there are thousands of them, succulent and creamy, their undersides a soft brown like pleated velvet. You have a taste for them now, but you opt for the safer option and buy some, frying them with garlic to have on toast.

At home there is much discussion about the heating.
Surely it's time?
No, not till November.
November! But it's practically winter already . . .
You stick to your guns, until one evening when you're alone in the house and the wind rattles the windows you

give in, flicking the switch and hearing the delicious click as the boiler fires.

You have raked the leaves from the garden into a pile in one corner for the hedgehogs, and collected a whole bag of conkers because someone once told you they keep away spiders. There is only one apple tree in your garden, but the grass is peppered with windfalls, and there are still hundreds more on the branches. You peel and core and chop and stew the fruit with cinnamon and sugar, to have on morning porridge. You make apple chutney, and apple tarts, and slow-dry rings in the oven overnight to store in glass jars, and still the boughs are heavy with more. You resort to putting buckets by the front door with a hand-written sign: *Free apples, please help yourself!*

Despite the vast leaves that rambled across the veg patch, you have failed to produce a single pumpkin. You buy one from Tesco – fat and orange, but with tasteless pale flesh no good for anything. On Hallowe'en the children draw wonky eyes and a toothy grimace with marker pen so you can cut away what isn't needed. You find candles from somewhere, and you wedge one inside and turn out the lights, and the children are amazed.

You sit the pumpkin by the front door; the bowl of sweets just inside. Ready.

Trick or treat?

Treat. It is always a treat.

Get the party started

After years of taking the children to birthday parties, and standing awkwardly at the back of the hall with a bunch of mums I barely knew, the day I was allowed to leave them there was a happy one indeed.

'Just jot your number down in case of problems,' the birthday boy's dad said. 'Pick them up at four?'

I was out of there so fast I left skid marks on the tarmac.

Nowadays it's more paint-balling and sleepovers than pirates and picnics, and apart from the last-minute panics over presents and cards, my children are pretty self-sufficient. This is perhaps less down to their enthusiasm to help and more about avoiding the sort of disaster I was prone to in the early years of parenting.

The party was being held at the village hall. It had been one of those frantic days where nothing had gone according to plan, and I was still picking the Rice Krispies out of my hair at lunchtime.

The invitation had been pinned to the noticeboard for a fortnight, during which time the children had demanded to see it on numerous occasions, amid much discussion about what they should wear and what Anna's present should be. The latter point was somewhat moot: Anna, like all children unfortunate enough to be friends with mine, would receive a gift from the under-stairs stash of presents my own children have been given but I haven't wanted them to keep.

I picked out something suitably girly and wrapped it up before the children could see and lay claim to it. Slotting them into their partywear I snatched up the invitation and hustled everyone out of the house, silently applauding myself for my timeliness.

When we arrived at the village hall, adorned with pink and white balloons, there were several children already hurling around the obligatory bouncy castle and parents congregating in the kitchen where plates of ham sandwiches had been cling-filmed into submission. I looked around for a familiar face and sighed when I recognised no one. That was the downside of having been a working mother for so long: I hadn't made the sort of school-gate acquaintances that prove so useful on occasions such as this.

Still, I was impressed to see that bottles of wine were uncorked on the side, and I helped myself to a large glass of red. Children's parties are significantly more tolerable when there is alcohol involved.

Sitting on a plastic chair by the side of the bouncy castle, I rifled in my bag for something to do and gave an idle glance over the party invitation, crumpled next to my purse. How odd, I thought, noticing the date. I could have sworn it was the 10th today, yet the invitation clearly said the 11th. I checked my diary, and as the truth dawned on me I took a large and rather panicked gulp of my wine.

We were at the wrong party.

What on earth was I to do? Parenting manuals were woefully lacking in this sort of practical advice. Should I gather up the children and try to slip out quietly? Impossible – just prising them off the bouncy castle would require an industrial tool of some sort. Identify the birthday girl's mother (she'd be the harassed one in the kitchen) and confess my mistake? Not a chance – it would be all over town before the weekend was out.

I decided to just brazen it out. After all, we'd already been there for half an hour and no one appeared to be whispering in corners, pointing at me. Besides, this wine was really rather good. I sauntered over to the bar and helped myself to a top-up, engaging another mother in conversation for a few minutes. *Yes, it is a lovely party. Yes, an awful lot of work. Yes, such a lovely cake.*

I wondered if we could do this every weekend. There always seemed to be a children's party on at the village hall, and it wasn't as though there was a guest list on the door . . .

Somebody called the children in for tea and I had a sudden pang of fear that there might not be enough chairs. Fortunately there seemed to be an abundance of places and my three uninvited guests settled into their sandwiches and cucumber sticks, chatting happily to the other children. I made a mental note to find out if they knew anyone there.

The cake arrived and a proud parent launched into 'Happy Birthday', to which I sung gaily along, coughing strategically and listening intently when we got to the birthday girl's name. Ah, so this was *Chloe's* party. I racked my brains but couldn't remember any of the children ever mentioning a Chloe.

As the birthday tea drew to a close and the party bags were dished out, I gathered the children and filed out with the others, thanking Chloe's mother for a wonderful party. I was jubilant. We had successfully crashed a four-year-old's birthday party and no one would ever be any the wiser.

Just as I was chuckling slightly to myself I remembered our gift, placed proudly on the present table with its tag neatly displayed.

With much love from the Mackintosh family – happy birthday, Anna.

Hallowe'en hater

The shops are filled with ghouls, zombies and pumpkin paraphernalia, and the children are positively beside themselves with excitement. Dressing up is second only to eating sweets on their list of Things We Enjoy, which makes Hallowe'en a veritable mecca.

There's just one tiny problem.

I hate it.

I suppose I'm fairly ambivalent about the fancy dress element (although fake blood's a bugger to get off the carpet), but trick or treat? Not a chance. I object as a matter of course to the Americanisation of British culture, which has seen us awash with school proms and options to 'supersize', and I draw the line at the legalised begging masquerading as a seasonal festivity. If the children want to dress up in white sheets, then so be it, but I refuse to let them knock on our neighbours' doors asking for sweets, particularly not when I've spent a significant amount of time hammering home to them the dangers of strangers laden with sweets (and puppies, although at Hallowe'en these are less of a risk than Haribo).

And don't get me started on the sinister side of Hallowe'en door-knocking. Up and down the country there are elderly or otherwise vulnerable people who are so terrified of the 'tricks' this time of year brings that they switch off their lights at 4 p.m. and sit in the dark, shaking at the sound of voices outside. Sure, I can make sure my own children aren't armed with eggs and flour, but by trick-or-treating they are perpetuating the whole horrid phenomenon.

I know – killjoy, right?

When the children were younger, Rob, who sees nothing wrong with a spot of harmless sweet-harvesting, decreed that on Hallowe'en the children could visit neighbours we knew well enough to ask in advance. I decreed they could not. We attempted to out-decree each other for a while, before coming to an uncomfortable compromise. The children could dress up and visit the neighbours to show them their costumes, but on no account would they utter the words 'trick or treat', and they would absolutely not ask for sweets.

In fact, I decided, we would *give* something instead, thereby doing our own tiny bit to reverse the hideousness of Hallowe'en. I whipped up a batch of treats while the children were turning themselves into the undead, and as soon as it got vaguely dark we began our tour of the street. It had all seemed such a good idea in my head, but I have to confess I felt faintly ridiculous as we chorused 'Happy Hallowe'en' in lieu of the traditional greeting.

'Oh goodness, what scary ghosts!' our elderly neighbour said.

The children beamed with pride and threw in a couple of ghostly *woooooo*s for good measure. The neighbour reached for an enormous basket of goodies by the front door and the children's eyes lit up.

'Oh, no thank you,' I said, producing my own cakes with a flourish. 'But would you care for a Hallowe'en flapjack?'

'Um . . . okay then.'

I felt she could have been a little more enthusiastic, to be honest. We bade her farewell and repeated the process a further three times before calling it a day.

'You see,' I said brightly, 'you *can* have fun without begging for sweets!'

Three pairs of eyes gazed dejectedly back at me from under their ghostly hoods. I offered them all a flapjack, and they chomped miserably as we made our way home.

In the cold light of the following day I realised my plan – while well-intentioned – was perhaps not wholly commendable. The children had me pegged as a mean old witch (how very seasonal), and the neighbours thought I was barking.

So I gave in.

Since then, at Hallowe'en the children have been allowed to dress up and run riot. They have wielded buckets to collect their ill-gotten stash, and throw rubber spiders at anyone brave enough to ask for a trick.

But they've done it with Dad: I stay home with the lights off and the curtains drawn.

Hallowe'en? Bah humbug.

Practice makes perfect

They say that ten thousand hours of consistent practice is sufficient to become an expert in almost anything. I beg to differ. By my estimation I have been practising parenting for more than ninety thousand hours; you'd think I'd be raking in the awards by now. Where is my Mother of the Year award? My Pretty Damn Good at Parenting trophy? Frankly, I'd settle for a Mediocre Mum badge. But nothing. Zip. Nada. Needless to say, my no-more-shouting resolution lasted little longer than the left-over Quality Street.

I have been mothering for over a decade (not including the hinter years of early marriage, featuring no children, but a husband fresh off the apron strings, which is practically the same thing) and I still suck at it. I have lost count of the number of times I have vowed to stop yelling, promised myself I'll play more games with the kids or help more with their homework. For years I've bookmarked ideas for creative play, cut baking recipes out of magazines and looked up how to make my own Play-Doh.

Have I made it? Have I hell. Time races by like someone's pressed fast-forward, and I barely have time to catch my breath before the next milestone whizzes past.

No sooner had I become an expert in dealing with toddler tantrums than someone crept in and moved the goalposts, and suddenly I had to know my times tables and be good at phonics. I turn my back for a second and the job description changes again. *How are your computer skills? When was Queen Victoria crowned? How do you get grass stains out of cricket whites?* I defy any head-hunter to find an applicant with the right transferable skills to be a parent.

Friends tell me to make the most of these years 'before teenage hormones hit', but already I can see them seeping into my erstwhile gentle children. A slammed door from the eleven-year-old; a pouty hand-on-hip from a ten-year-old seconds away from another strop. Testosterone and oestrogen hang in the air like a mushroom cloud. Thank goodness there are two of us.

The Big House Move has been accompanied by a Big Move on the domestic front. Rob has followed in my footsteps and left the thin blue line. For the first time in our family life he is home at weekends and during the evenings, he's there for the school pick-up, and for home-work and teatime. And boy am I glad of it. Not only because I can write uninterrupted, but because if there's one area of motherhood in which I truly, madly, deeply suck, it's homework.

Oh, sure, I can help with the essay-writing, the spellings, and the addition of 'wow words' (adjectives to you and me) to a piece of prose, but present me with a maths quandary and Houston: we have a problem.

'That's an interesting one,' I'll stall, pretending to scan

the exercise book thrust under my nose. 'Why don't you have a go at working it out on your own, before I tell you what the answer is?'

At which point I'll retreat to the downstairs loo with a scrap of paper, a calculator and Google, before emerging triumphantly with the result. Heaven knows what parents did before Google. It's my go-to resource for everything from bedwetting and medical complaints to gymnastic tutorials and origami instructions. I'm adept at searching; sifting through the adverts to find a reliable source and pinging a link to myself for future reference.

If I've spent ninety thousand hours parenting, then I must have spent at least a tenth of that time looking things up on Google.

Almost ten thousand searches: I guess I could call myself an expert.

Aga saga

I have always dreamed of having an Aga. Long before I reached an age where interior magazines and *Cotswold Life* subscriptions could have planted the idea in my head, I pined for a kitchen built around one of these classic beasts. Agas featured heavily in my favourite books – almost exclusively about ponies, or boarding schools (or both) – where the warming oven would be permanently occupied by sickly lambs or labrador pups (or both). My fictional counterparts would wake early for Pony Club rallies to find their jodhpurs warming on the rail; mine would be crumpled at the bottom of my laundry basket where I left them. By this stage the Aga had acquired such magical properties that I was able to gloss over my own contribution to such domestic fails, and instead point the finger towards my family's short-sightedness in installing a modern kitchen.

On visits to my friend Caroline, I would lean casually on her parents' Aga, feeling the warmth through my school uniform and imagining curling up in an armchair next to it to do my homework. It would surely improve my concentration, my creativity, my ability to understand algebra . . .

As I grew up, my obsession waned to a more manageable level. I managed not to blame my lack of Aga for love, laundry or career fails, and when the time came for my husband and I to buy our first home, I realised swiftly that – in the Cotswolds, at least – the sort of house that came with an Aga was not the sort of house in budget for two public-sector workers with a minimal deposit. We bought a house. We bought another, two years later. Moved again, a few years after that.

Still no Aga.

I had put it behind me, just as I had put to one side other childhood obsessions such as My Little Pony, *Top of the Pops* and a refusal to go anywhere without my own pillow (still a work in progress, that one). It wasn't until I had children that my love for Agas blossomed anew, sparked by the sight of Babygros drying on an airer suspended from the ceiling in the farmhouse kitchen of an NCT friend.

Oh, if only I had an Aga! No more damp muslin cloths draped over radiators. No more soggy bibs waiting for the tumble dryer. I imagined the ease with which I could warm my baby's bottle, or defrost those tiny pots of pureed mush. No wonder we had tears at bathtime, with no warm towels fresh from the Aga . . .

My online house-hunting expeditions began to acquire a new focus. I clicked swiftly away from any kitchen not sporting a cast-iron cooker and cursed Rightmove for not offering a 'Has an Aga' filter option. Who cared about off-street parking, a fourth bedroom or semi-detached status? It was all about the Aga.

And now it's finally happening. The new house *has an Aga*. I am impossibly excited.

An Aga!

It will keep my tea warm in the morning as I run up and down stairs, chivvying the children. It'll dry our laundry and heat our water. We'll defrost chilly fingers after a winter's snowball fight, and hang up our swimsuits after a dip in the river.

The Aga will be the heart of the home.

There's just one thing: how the hell do I cook on it?

Pet detective

The children want a pet. Pets, to be precise. Oh, I know, we already have the dog (on which they dote), but they want something small and furry, and as the new house will give us more space I've given in. The question is, what to get?

There's a gap in the market for a pet-matching service: a dating agency where expert petologists assess your needs and find you the perfect companion. Single, but like to chat? Get a parrot. Insomniac? Gerbils are nocturnal. Allergic to fur? Easy: you want a tortoise.

Here in the Mackintosh household, there has been much clamouring for a kitten.

'You know they don't stay kittens for long?' we said. The children vowed to love a cat even once it was old and crotchety, but nevertheless it was a no from us. I love cats. They're cuddly, independent and easy to look after. I'm less fond of their habit of bringing in mice, chasing them around the house and then depositing the semi-live remains upon their master's bed. See also: shredding the furniture, climbing the curtains and using the plant pots as litter trays (my mother's African violets never recovered), not to mention their ability to turn any outfit into a furry bathmat within minutes. Rob and I were resolute: no cats.

George's optimistic longing for a tarantula was pretty short-lived (shiver), as was Josh's suggestion of rats (seriously?), and Evie's plea for a sugar glider that would accompany her everywhere in a specially made pouch (I have to admit I wavered. Have you seen them? Ridiculously cute).

'Why do we need more pets anyway?' Rob grumbled as I measured up the new playroom for a terrarium.

It was a fair point. I grew up with dogs, cats, rabbits, guinea pigs, goldfish and horses. A house is never quite a home, for me, without at least one of the above, and ideally all of them. As for *need* . . .

'It teaches the children responsibility,' I said.

I winced at a sudden memory of my mother telling me off for leaving her to clean out Sooty's hutch *again*.

In fact, now I think about it, didn't my mum end up looking after the guinea pigs as well? And wasn't she the one who scraped the algae off the inside of the fish tank, remembered to buy pondweed and flushed the fish that didn't make it? And wasn't it her who pushed worming tablets into wedges of cheese and pulled frankly unrecognisable socks from the nether regions of a cairn terrier? Best I don't mention any of that to Rob.

'Something small, then,' he sighed. 'Something that can live outdoors.'

We held a family conference. By which I mean I mentioned it at supper.

'Chickens?' I said optimistically. I was already missing them.

'They're not pets!' cried the children.

'We've had chickens,' said Rob, as though that ruled us out from ever having them again.

'How about guinea pigs?' I said. I have a certain fondness for guinea pigs, with their funny little ears and cute squeaking noises, and not-at-all-bikini-ready bodies. Less bitey than rabbits (as a child, I kept a pair of gardening gloves handy for when Sooty was feeling particularly grumpy), but just as straightforward to look after.

'Yes!' the children chorused. 'Guinea pigs!'

'Oh, okay,' said the husband, somewhat grumpily.

Guinea pigs it is, then. I wonder how long before it's my turn to clean them out.

NOVEMBER

In November, the trees are standing all sticks and bones. Without their leaves, how lovely they are, spreading their arms like dancers. They know it is time to be still.

Cynthia Rylant

Without their summer dresses the winter trees are stark against the sky. Through their naked limbs you see the curve of the hills and the shape of the hedgerow. Robbed of their leafy shelters, the birds hide instead in tree trunks and walls, and in the ivy that takes no notice of cold winds or icy rain.

Bonfires are built and lit, crackling with autumn leaves and casting a golden glow on children's faces. They wave sparklers, fizzing in the air, and you watch them try to write their names – the first letter fading before the last has been made. There are baked potatoes, crisp in their skins and wrapped in foil – as welcome to keep your hands warm as they are to eat – and mugs of parsnip soup with sprinklings of crispy bacon.

When the fireworks begin you retreat to the house, worried about the animals. The dog is asleep, and the cat unperturbed, but you stay indoors anyway, enjoying the interlude away from the others. From here, the bangs and pops are muted – the crackles and fizzes easier on the ear – and the colours in the sky are framed by the sitting-room window, like a painting hung for a private viewing.

They go off one by one at first – rockets and flares and comets – and you smile at the *oohs* and *aahs* that follow each one; and then two fly at once, and then three, and then more, faster and faster and faster. It is, you know, leading to the grand finale: the super-duper giant flare that shoots to the moon then spins and whirls and dissolves into a million tiny stars. The culmination of much discussion, of much of the evening's budget. *It has to be perfect* has been the constant refrain – *for the children*.

Silence falls outside. This is the moment, you know – you have been privy to the stage directions. A drum-roll begins, a countdown from ten. *Seven, six, five* . . . You watch from your window. *Three, two, one* . . .

There is a muffled pop, and a pathetic burst of bright pink dots that fall into nothing the moment they appear.

The fireworks display is over.

You try not to laugh, because you know they will be disappointed, but honestly, isn't it always the way? And when you join them again, outside, the finale is forgotten and another round of sparklers has been lit, and you stand in the darkness, hugging happiness to yourself.

Body magic

Remember how I said I didn't do dieting support groups? Well, I've had to eat my words (along with the cream buns, the buttered toast and the bags of crisps that got me into this predicament in the first place . . .). Dieting alone just wasn't doing it: I've joined Fat Club. That's not what it's called, obviously ('It's not a diet, ladies, it's a way of life'), but that's what it is. Twenty-or-so overweight women (and one man; there's always a man, and he always loses weight twice as fast as all the women put together, thanks to the very male trait of single-mindedness, and the absence of that very female trait, chocolate addiction), lining up once a week to be congratulated on a half-pound loss and jollied out of despair when the scales tip the other way.

I joined under duress.

Mine. I was – well, if not fat exactly, certainly fatter than I wanted to be. I clearly lacked the willpower to stick to any kind of diet at home, and the constant travelling and eating out (such a hardship, I know) meant many of my meals were out of my control. Something had to give; and if I didn't tackle it, it was likely to be my trousers. Friends had waxed lyrical about the difference this particular group had made to their lives, and I was an avid follower on Instagram of successful devotees (#myslimmingjourney #eatclean #cheatday #pies #dreamingaboutcreambuns #hashtag #hashtag #hashtag). I was ready to give it a go.

The *Oxford English Dictionary* defines the word 'cult' as *a particular form or system of religious worship or veneration, especially as expressed in ceremony or ritual directed towards a specified figure or object* – a definition entirely familiar if you've ever encountered a dieter with a shopping basket full of Müller Light yoghurts. As I swiftly learned, Fat Club devotees whisk Müller Lights into puddings. They turn them into cake frosting. They make muffins with them. And guess what the secret ingredient is in a Fat Club egg pudding . . . yup, Müller Light.

Look, I like yoghurt. Just not *that* much. When Fat Club members aren't cooking with Müller Light, they're cooking with quark; an ingredient I'd never heard of before January this year, and which now appears in 50 per cent of my recipes (the other 50 per cent involve yoghurt). Like any good cult, indoctrination requires memorising an entire dictionary of new words. You don't 'diet', you 'food optimise'; 'free' foods still cost money; and – my personal favourite – taking a brisk walk isn't 'exercise', but 'Body Magic'. Cringe.

In short, as you can probably tell, I embarked upon my Fat Club #journey with no small degree of scepticism. I was positively *willing* it to fail.

It didn't.

In fact, I've loved it. I still baulk at using the jargon

('Any Body Magic this week, Clare?' trills my cult leader. 'No, but I've been to the gym three times') and I refuse to accept that a Diet Coke's better for you than an avocado and a dollop of extra virgin olive oil, but other than that I'm a fully paid up (£4.95 every week, whether I show up or not – that's enough of an incentive on its own) member of the Fat Club clan. A stone and a half down, and I'm on the final lap. Two measly pounds to go, and I can stop dieting ('It's not a diet, it's a way of life . . .') and become a Target Member.

Yes: there's a special name for it. Of course there is. Free membership for life . . . just as long as you stay within sniffing distance of your ideal weight. And therein lies the rub, given my propensity to put on weight if I so much as look in the general direction of a sausage roll.

You mean I have to eat like this *for ever*?

Don't get me wrong: the recipes are delicious (Mac'n'cheesey quark, anyone?) and following the plan is as easy as pie (mmm, pie . . .), but oh my goodness I miss proper chips, and flaky pastry, and piles of buttered toast, and lounging on my hotel bed with the room service menu and a craving for deep-fried Camembert . . . I know what my cult leader will suggest.

'Everything in moderation, and lots of Body Magic to keep a balance.'

Magic? To stand a cat in hell's chance of competing with my cravings it'll need to be fuelled by Dumbledore himself. Still, I'm almost there. I feel great; my clothes fit; and the seams on my trousers are breathing a sigh of relief.

After all, as Kate Moss famously pointed out, nothing tastes as good as skinny feels.

Well, almost nothing.

Anyone know if you can make deep-fried Camembert from Müller Light yoghurt and quark?

Go go gadgets

The children have been given iPods. They were supposed to be Christmas presents, but have been delivered early in order to ease the move from one school to another, by facilitating regular contact with their old friends.

I held out for as long as I could – despite my own internet addiction I am not a fan of screen time – but the house move seemed an ideal opportunity to introduce them. After all, we have now entered the world of secondary school, where phones are now practically compulsory, so it's a good time to practise some personal responsibility.

The rules are simple.

Break it: pay for it.

Lose it: pay for it.

So far, so careful. It will come as no surprise that they have taken to this new technology like ducks to water. None of the inept fumbling I remember from my first foray into the iPhone cult; not for them the fat-fingered errors or the accidental swipes, the squinting at the screen and the reluctant but inevitable Google search for How to Increase Font Size on your iPhone. Today's youth are born with touch capabilities quite literally at their fingertips. Give a two-year-old an iPad and he will confidently scroll through Peppa Pig images, navigate YouTube and take covert photos of Daddy on the loo to post on Instagram.

Within minutes of handing my three children their much-coveted iPods, I was treated to a masterclass of functions that my many years as an Apple owner had failed to reveal.

'So, um, how did you do that?' I asked Josh, as he played me a photographic slideshow complete with soundtrack.

'Easy!' he proclaimed, fingers whizzing across the screen as he replicated the slideshow for me.

And then it dawned on me: I've become the Older Generation. Incapable of setting a TV programme to record without assistance from someone born after 2000, and ignoring six out of seven of the cycles on the dishwasher because I don't know what they mean. Before too long I'll be saying 'in my day' and tutting about modern music being nothing but noise.

It's not as though I'm a complete Luddite; I'm a social media devotee, after all, and there's barely a corner of the internet I haven't explored in the name of pleasure, procrastination or book research. On trains I whip out my Bluetooth keyboard, pair it with my phone and tap out a quick column. My Fitbit chirpily vibrates when I've reached that day's step target, and you'd never see me on a plane without my Kindle.

I embrace technology.

I love it.

It's just that nowadays I don't always understand it.

And so the children take on the tech baton and run
with it, with no comprehension of how much has changed
even in their own short lifetimes; that they hold in their
hands a tiny device ten times more powerful than the
huge desktop computer I took to university, which whirred
and chugged as it processed the simplest of documents,
and took two full minutes to dial up a connection to the
World Wide Web.

How quickly we have learned to take it for granted;
how fast we discover we could not function without it.
For my children, everything is there at the touch of a
button. Phone numbers, opening hours, train times, shopping, films, games, email, video conferencing . . . Little
wonder they clamoured so long for these tiny, shiny
gadgets. No wonder they cling to them as though they
have been grafted to their palms.

'No screens before school,' I remind them. 'No screens
until homework's done. No screens in bed.'

'Put it away *now*,' I said somewhat impatiently to Evie
the other day, as I caught a glimpse of shimmering glass
from where she sat in the playroom.

'But I need it!' she insisted, leaning forward protectively.
I sighed, and braced myself for an argument. 'Look!' she
said.

I looked. And found a house, built from books, a ruler
and a collection of playing cards. Inside, her Sylvanian
Families characters were grouped in the kitchen around
a make-believe tea. The table? Evie's iPod, upside down
and balanced carefully on four Lego blocks.

'Can they just finish their supper?' she asked.

'Of course they can,' I said, sitting down beside her to join in.

Gadgets are great, but nothing beats a bit of good old-fashioned fun.

Making waves

For many years, I was a terrible swimmer. Terrified of putting my head in the water, I completed the obligatory twenty-five-metre assessed swim of my childhood only on the hard-bargained promise of pickled onion crisps and the immediate cessation of lessons if I passed. I did, and so began more than twenty years of swimming like a duck, head protruding from the water while my limbs paddled furiously beneath the surface. I would gaze enviously at the sleek swimmers in the fast lane, cutting through the water like hot knives through butter, while I – and the old ladies of the parish – performed sedate breaststroke in amongst the armbands and the woggles.

In the changing rooms afterwards I'd join in with the surreptitious circling of stiff necks, and wonder if all this exercise is really worth it if I end up with muscles so taut I'll have to look up at the sky when I talk to people. Still, it was hardly a pressing issue, and if it meant I had to pick up the odd dropped locker key with my toes instead of ducking beneath the surface to retrieve it, so be it. I would pride myself on my dextrous monkey-toes instead of my diving skills. To each their own talents.

It wasn't until my children were learning to swim that I gave my phobia of water a second thought.

'Face in the water,' I'd instruct between lessons, determined to add an educational element to our Saturday-morning splashabout.

'I don't like it,' George would say.

Evie was more astute. 'Why don't you show us, Mummy?'

She would smile sweetly, knowing full well I would no more sink my head into the water than I would run willingly into a burning building. What kind of mother was I? This was no example to set to impressionable young people. Here I was, trying to ensure my children were confident, safe and happy in the water, and all the while I was flinching every time a drop splashed my cheek. I had to beat this. I started small – in the shower, where rivulets of warm water on my face had always brought on a near panic attack – and progressed to the swimming pool, late at night when no one swam but me. The water was still. So was I, mostly, actual *swimming* being a bridge too far at that stage. Instead I crouched in the shallow end, sinking my face into the water by infinitesimal degrees, before slowly starting to blow bubbles the way I had watched my children learn to do.

It took weeks. Months. It was only afterwards that I realised the (unsupervised) pool was monitored via CCTV by the reception staff, to whom it must have looked suspiciously as though I was having a wee. However, by the following spring I could swim a length of proper breaststroke, breathing out underwater and surfacing only to inhale. I was euphoric. Swimming no longer gave me neck ache, made me feel ridiculous or kept my heart rate too low to be useful. Proper swimming was hypnotic, almost meditative. Before too long I was addicted; slipping into the pool even if I only had five minutes to spare, just for the blissful endorphins it released.

I began to yearn to swim somewhere without lifeguards and lanes; where chlorine didn't sting my eyes, and naked ladies didn't invade my personal space in the changing rooms. Somewhere, in fact, with no changing rooms at all . . .

Wild swimming. Even the name is exciting.

My wetsuit was a birthday present from Rob, thus cementing my commitment to open-water swimming. I was temporarily discombobulated to discover I'd be sporting the word Orca across my bosom, as I already felt distinctly whale-like when squeezed into unforgiving rubber, but I quickly rallied and went for my first dip.

Open-water swimming is a world away from pool swimming – whether indoors or out. I floated on my back that first time (wetsuits provide useful buoyancy) and gazed up at the sky, and knew that this was the start of a beautiful relationship.

Since then I've swum in sunshine and in rain, alone and with friends. I've swum in the dark, as the sun peeks over the horizon, and when tendrils of mist dance across the surface of the lake. I've swum when the ice is cracking between the pebbles on the shore, and the water's so cold it feels like a burn on bare skin. It is gloriously, crazily exhilarating, and I'm grateful to my children for unwittingly giving me the impetus to love swimming.

Mind you, I'm looking forward to summer. I got out four hours ago and I still can't feel my toes.

Bully for you

Hardly a week passes without some mention in the paper of the risk of bullying, both cyber and real-life, for today's children. As Josh settles into secondary school I'm alert to the signs – reluctance to go to school, lack of socialising, loss of appetite – and relieved to see none to date.

I was fortunate to survive my own childhood with little more than a gentle joshing about the colour of my hair (strawberry blond; never red, and *definitely* never ginger) and the elongated nature of my vowels back then, in words like 'plastic' and 'elastic'. I never fell in with one particular set, yet neither was I kept out of one, and so I wandered through school and university making friends and moving on from them without any drama.

Motherhood, I was told: that's when the cliques really form. The stay-at-home mums versus the work-full-timers; the co-sleepers versus the let-them-criers; the feed-on-demands versus the Gina Fords: such are the divides that define us. I didn't find it so. My peers were curious about one another's parenting styles, not judgemental. *Whatever works for you*, they said; *everyone's different*, they said. As the children grew I wondered about the myth of the school-gate mafia, and felt almost disappointed by its absence. I braced myself for cliques and comparisons, but found instead tolerant parents who celebrated each other's successes. Where was the bitchiness? Where were the whispers in corners, the pointed looks, and the damning sartorial stares I'd been promised by the *Guardian* family section?

I moved from reception to Key Stage One and beyond without incident; crept towards the end of primary school . . . and then – WHAM!

'Hello,' I said as I passed a fellow parent at pick-up time. Silence. I shrugged it off. Preoccupied, perhaps, with another note from school, the demands of yet another after-school club. A hearing problem, previously undisclosed. Myriad reasons. That it had been intentional never crossed my mind, until Facebook – the cause of so much angst it should really come with a health warning – informed me that such was the case.

Some people are so fake! I read.

I rolled my eyes at the dog. Who was today's target of her passive aggression, I wondered? I read on.

Someone said hello but it was obvious they didn't mean it.

Oh. Not preoccupied, then. Not a hearing problem. Quite deliberate. I contemplated her accusation, trying to establish exactly what part of hello I hadn't meant. I thought of the numerous pub fights I'd been to in my police days, allegedly started because someone looked at someone else funny. At least my own adversary was unlikely to break a bottle over my head.

An online conversation ensued, in which a dozen anxious women sought to establish whether their own hellos had been sufficiently sincere, and were reassured that yes indeed, whatever authenticity was required in those two syllables had indeed been delivered. I double-checked to make sure I was actually reading an adult's Facebook updates, and hadn't stumbled inadvertently into a toddler's playground.

And then it came: the invisible punch to the stomach.

You probably know who I mean! she wrote, prompting a series of LOLs and winking faces. I'm not ashamed to admit that it made me cry. Protected by the internet, I jumped into the discussion with a faux-jolly comment: *Hey, what's going on? I said hello, you ignored me – have I offended you somehow?*

She blocked me.

End of conversation. The last word. Oscar Wilde proclaimed that the only thing worse than being talked about was not being talked about. I wonder how often he did the school run. I wonder if he'd want to do it now, in the knowledge that the pack can round so quickly on one woman. A woman who said hello with the wrong sort of emphasis. A woman minding her own business; a head full of books to write, articles to file, PE kits to find, dentist appointments to book, suppers to make; who gives no more thought to the way she says hello than she does to tying her shoelaces or taking a breath.

I didn't do the school run the next day. I didn't want to.

Who else thought I said hello without the necessary sincerity? Who else would I find talking about me on Facebook, deliberately baiting me from behind the safety of a screen?

Paranoia quickly turned to anger, and then from anger to the sweetest of all reactions: laughter.

How absurd! How ridiculous! I sang as I drove the children to school, chirruping my 'Hello!' loudly enough for the whole playground to hear. Slowly and deliberately she turned her back on me.

'Have a wonderful day!' I cried through the car window as I drove away.

She didn't respond. Neither did she appear to appreciate the jazz hands that accompanied the following day's hello, or my husband's booming greeting when it was his turn for the school run. Sincere hellos are clearly hard to pull off. I could continue my efforts, but life is too short. For every one person who wants to pick an imaginary fight, there are dozens more who don't.

I'll save my hellos, in all their distracted, but sincere, glory, for them.

Field work

As moving day approaches, there has been much debate over what to do with the field that comes with the new house. A little less than an acre, it lies to the immediate rear of the long, hedge-lined back garden, accessed via a metal five-bar gate with dropped hinges, too heavy for the children to lift. The current residents are two dozen or more woolly sheep; the property of a farmer a few doors down, who has tenanted this same field for more than twenty years and is hopeful to continue the arrangement. It is difficult to say no, and so we will no doubt take the too-few ten-pound notes for it to be worth our while, and remind ourselves of the hours we'll save in tending the field and he's doing us a favour really, isn't he? But the field belongs to the house, and at some point in the future we will reclaim it. But for what purpose?

'A pony!' cried Evie as we sat amid packing crates with mugs of tea.

'Too small,' I replied. She scowled.

'Me? Or the field?'

'Both.'

I have plans for the field, and they don't include poo-picking once a week and scouring the undergrowth for ragwort. The field is perfect for an orchard. Neat rows of apple trees; clusters of pears. Long trestle tables covered with crisp French linen, groaning with salads and cheeses for hungry harvesters. We could produce our own cider; I'll make jams by the bucketload to fill the cellar I suspect I will be too scared to venture into.

'We could rescue a donkey,' Rob said. I looked at my husband. 'Or a goat.'

I softened slightly, distracted from my fantasy orchard. Imagined an Eeyore, grazing on thistles; a pair of billy goats doing whatever billy goats do. They'd certainly take care of the grass, and the children would adore them. We could milk them!

Just in time, I remembered that attempting to milk a billy goat would definitely mark us out as newbies among the locals. I do love goat's cheese, though, so the idea of goats definitely had potential. Would the children embrace goat's milk on their cornflakes, I wondered?

I sat bolt upright, inspiration striking. Alpacas!

'What do they do?' Rob said in response to my brilliant idea. I racked my brains; remembered the gorgeous scarf I received last Christmas.

'They have super-soft coats. We'd shear them,' – I was a little hazy on the detail – 'then I'd knit from the wool.'

Rob looked dubious. 'Remember that jumper you made me?' The sweater in question had one arm shorter than the other, and so many dropped stitches I'd had to pass off the design as lace. Maybe not alpacas, then.

'Could we have a football pitch?' George wanted to know. 'It would be less poo-ey than goats or alpac-wotsits.'

I looked at Rob. That would be easy enough. A couple of goals and Bob's your uncle. Or in this case, your dad.

'And we could have floodlights for when it's dark,' George continued, 'and a manager's box and stands for home and away, and—'

Clearly George had a rather more ambitious image in mind than my two-goals-and-a-can-of-white-spray-paint plan.

'What do *you* think we should do with the field?' I asked Josh, who had yet to throw an idea into the ring. He rolled his eyes; a teenager in the making.

'Why do we have to *do* anything with it?'

Honestly, children . . .

'Well,' I said, as patiently as I could, 'because it will be *ours*. We'll own it. So we can do what we want with it. We could have a rescue donkey, or goats, or alpacas, or an amazing orchard with white linen tablecloths on rustic trestle tables . . .'

I broke off as Josh's eyes glazed over. Did no one else in this family have any vision?

He looked at me with an expression that was becoming increasingly familiar. 'Don't you think you're busy enough, Mummy, without adding goats and donkeys to your list?'

I resisted the urge to punch the air as my boy played unwittingly into my hands. 'Perhaps you're right,' I said sadly. 'I guess an orchard would be best after all.' I caught the glance between my children and their father. 'What?'

There was a long pause.

'We were just remembering the time you made marmalade.'

Ah yes. Marmalade-gate. Litres of orange goo, bravely poured into sterilised jars in the hope that it would somehow set of its own accord. It did not. For months I poured it like honey onto anything and everything, until even I grew sick of it and bagged it up for the bin men. Apples would be different, though. Cider, and dried apple rings, and apple compote, and . . . I sighed. Looked around the table.

'We'll just keep the sheep, shall we?' I said.

My husband nodded. 'That's the best idea you've had yet.'

Learning the language

I can't help but feel life was easier before the children learned to read. Far be it from me to stem the tide of education, but it's terribly awkward having to hide things from view. Gone are the days when I could leave suggestive notes for my husband in red lipstick on the bathroom mirror, or caustic quips on the fridge about bins that *don't put themselves out, you know*. I cannot now scribble ideas for Christmas presents on the kitchen board, leave rude knock-knock jokes on the iPad, or scrawl 'kill me now' across the *Radio Times* listing for *Strictly Come Dancing*. Every shopping list, every note for the cleaner, every milkman-message is deciphered out loud, with varying degrees of accuracy.

'Who are you buying a Slime Factory for?' cried Evie with excitement. 'I've wanted one of those for AGES!'

She bounced around the kitchen in some form of victory dance. I snatched the Post-it note from the kettle, where I had left it in a vain attempt to remind me that I absolutely, definitely, totally had to start my Christmas shopping.

'It's for me,' I said.

Her face fell. 'Really?'

I nodded. 'I need it for work.'

Evie sloped off, dismayed by this discovery and seem-ingly uninterested in why my work might require me to buy a collection of ingredients to make slime.

Round one to me: the children might be able to read, but they're still gullible.

Such is the enthusiasm for reading among my tribe that any word which stays still long enough will be spelt out with slow but furious concentration.

'Wh–ot–a–wuh–a–n–k– urr,' George said, several years ago, peering over my shoulder at a supportive text message I was sending to an irate friend.

I pressed delete and wrote 'Quel cochon!' instead. Thus French became my encryption of choice over the next few years, albeit a sort of hybrid code that finds a home somewhere between Rob's schoolboy franglais and my own half-forgotten fluency.

'Il faut acheter du vin – les enfants sont vachement horribles!' I'll text, hoping to divert him to the off-licence on his way home.

'Oui,' he will reply. 'Mais tu devrais pas drink it all, tu vieux soak.'

I can only assume the message loses some of intended subtlety in translation. In time, of course, as les enfants progress through school, this communication channel too will be thwarted, and I will be forced to learn Esperanto, but for now our Gallic missives are safe from the inquis-itive minds of three children.

It simply isn't practical, however, to write absolutely everything in French, and as the kids quite often head to my office in search of paper and sticky tape, I realise I shall have to be more circumspect about what I leave lying around.

'I've just read the start of *I Let You Go*, Mummy,' Josh said the other day, when he trotted downstairs with the Sellotape and my good scissors. Ever kind-hearted, he added encouragingly, 'It was very good.'

I hesitated. The prologue of my first novel begins with a rather traumatic hit-and-run, in which a young boy is killed. It's dark, gritty, and somewhat different to *Five Go Off in a Caravan*.

'Are you okay?' I asked. I wondered if the graphic description of a child rolling off the bonnet of a car would give my beautiful son nightmares, and I hoped I wouldn't spend the rest of my life shelling out for therapists.

'Yes,' Josh said, 'although there is one thing . . .' He broke off, looking a little worried.

'Oh, darling,' I said, dropping down to my knees so I could look him in the eye, 'it's really not meant for children to read. I'm so sorry if it upset you.'

'It's not that,' Josh said. He took a deep breath, clearly preparing me for bad news. 'I just think you need to use more adjectives.'

Quel petit vilain!

DECEMBER

O Christmas tree, o Christmas tree!
How lovely are your branches.

Christmas carol

There must be more to December than Christmas, but it is hard to find it beneath the preparations for what – as you keep having to remind yourself – is *only one day of the year*. There are lists to write, and gifts to choose and wrap, and food to plan and make ahead of time. You have promised mince pies for late-night shopping, and a fruit cake for the fayre, and somehow you've agreed to organise the carol-singing, even though you really can't hold a tune.

Signs by the roadside offer *Christmas geese* and *birds-in-birds*, and *Ostrich steaks – why not try something new?* You will stick to turkey, which you'll buy from the butcher, who keeps his queue happy on Christmas Eve with chocolate mints and tiny shots of sherry. You'll do pigs in blankets, of course, and too many potatoes, and sprouts to divide opinion. You'll dig out your wedding china, and use the best glasses, and hope the others won't forget they're bringing cheese.

On the first Saturday of the month you choose the

tree. It is a serious affair, every member of the family with a view on which is best. Taller than the tallest child – that's always been the rule, even though the smallest child is taller than you now. The right type of needles, the right colour green; the right-sized trunk to fit in at least one of the dozen stands you've acquired over the years. And only when it's been wrapped in net, and you've dragged it outside, do you wonder how you're ever going to get it in the car.

As the month goes by, and festive fever grows, you escape the madness and head for the hills. You forget your lists, and the Christmas cards you still haven't written, and the last delivery date, which you have no doubt missed. You march and you march, so fast you are soon too hot in your winter coat and your layers of fleece. You pull off your scarf and let it dangle beside you, but you don't stop until you reach the very top.

Sprawled out below, beneath the fields and the woodland, are a hundred houses filled with families just like yours. Christmas-ready and Christmas-not-so-ready; Christmas-keen and Christmas-not-so-keen. With twinkling lights, and full fridges, and stockings stashed ready for morning. All ready for a Cotswold Christmas.

Mother Christmas

Ever since the autumn leaves began dropping from the trees, there has only really been one topic of conversation in our house: Father Christmas. 'How many more sleeps till Father Christmas comes?'

'What do you think he'll bring us?'

'Will he know I've moved bedrooms?'

Frankly, it's starting to annoy me. Because, let's face it, who do you think is *really* the one putting together flat-pack toys, packing stockings, tying ribbons round parcels and making sure everything gets to the right place at the right time?

That's right: Mother Christmas.

While Santa sits on the sofa watching *Game of Thrones* and farting, Mother Christmas is flat out making minia-ture plum puddings, counting satsumas, and wondering if she's ever going to get time to shave her legs. Come December, Father Christmas has done nothing about Christmas (unless you count the LED snowman he bought because it was on special offer at the garage when he was putting diesel in the sleigh) and he sees nothing wrong with leaving it to the last minute. If confronted, he'll tell you it makes the whole affair 'more exciting'. 'More challenging'. Even, one year, 'more Christmassy'.

Left to his own devices, Old Beardy would start thinking about presents a week or so before Christmas, increasing the elves' workload to such an extent the union would step in and propose a vote of no confidence. They'd all go on strike and Mr Christmas would end up having to order the whole lot from Amazon (at twice the price, with dented boxes and missing the instructions).

Oh no, it's Mother Christmas we should be thanking. First in the queue for the January sales, she's the sort of woman who takes her sleeping bag to Gap for the Boxing Day sales, and leaves triumphantly clutching armfuls of bargains. Christmas is constantly on her mind, and she's sensible enough to spread the cost throughout the year: chocolate coins and sugar mice are tacked on to the weekly shop; souvenir pens and pencil sharpeners are snaffled for pennies and stashed away under the bed ready for the big day.

Mrs Christmas has everything under control. Not only does she know what everyone wants, she sources it all at the best price (thanks to her love of online comparison sites, and her subscription to *Which?* magazine) and has it delivered well before the risk of December postal delays. There's still lots to be made in-house, of course, but Mother Christmas wins out here, too. Motivating and supportive, she's already set out her expectations during the mid-year appraisals: even the union reps are on her side, thanks to a judicious gift of cinnamon shortbread. Home-made, of course.

The factory floor is buzzing, everyone's singing carols: Mother Christmas might even allow herself a small gin and tonic. No risk of missing their own celebrations, either: after that awful year when Father Christmas was in charge of the turkey and they all ended up eating pizza from the freezer because he'd forgotten to order it, Mrs C is firmly in control of the kitchen. The Ocado slot was booked in September (complete with free bottle of bubbly), and the crackers are from that nice place in Lechlade where it's Christmas all year round. The turkey's safely in the freezer (she's set a reminder on her phone to take it out two days before), and although she's never quite sure what to do with the giblets she's fairly certain Nigella will have a recipe.

In short, everything is going like clockwork.

So what's Father Christmas doing, against this whirlwind of activity? Feeling a little guilty? Offering to give her a hand? Perhaps he's shaking his head in admiration and saying I just don't know how you do it, my love . . .

No, he's down the pub. Everyone buys him a pint – of course they do, he's Father Christmas – and asks him how he's getting on with this year's preparations.

'Oh, it's all under control,' he smiles reassuringly. 'I've been doing it for so long I hardly think about it.'

And perhaps then he'll feel a pang of guilt when he thinks of the missus, up all night stuffing stockings.

'She enjoys it,' he'll mutter to himself, and the funny thing is, he's probably right. Mrs Christmas might be knackered, and slightly the worse for wear from gin, and she never did get round to shaving her legs . . . but really, she wouldn't have it any other way.

Keeping the secret

Whatever my thoughts on the inadequacies of Father Christmas, I dreaded the day the children stopped believing in him, and braced myself for the inevitable challenge. What would I say? How would I answer? This time of year is magical even without Father Christmas, of course: the nativity, snow, decorations, food, gifts . . . but for me Santa is the icing on the Christmas cake. How can anyone fail to smile at the sight of a big white beard, a cheery wave, a red suit and a 'ho, ho, ho'?

When children are very tiny – perhaps until they are three or four – they do not fully appreciate the magic. They wake up on Christmas morning and there are presents, and they're delighted by them, but it isn't until they are just a fraction older that you see the wide-eyed wonder as they realise *he has actually been*. Here, *in this room*! It is the stuff of fairy tales, and it is *actually happening to them right now*. Somehow, Father Christmas has read the letter so painstakingly written all those weeks ago by a small boy with his tongue poking out of the corner of his mouth. He has read that letter, found the perfect toys, and transported them by reindeer across the globe to *this very bedroom*. It is magic beyond their wildest dreams, and they enjoy it for such a short time, before they are hit by the age of disbelief.

Once there they will question the icing-sugar footprints, the raisin reindeer-droppings, the half-eaten mince pie, and they will laugh as their parents cling desperately on to the memories of Christmas Past. We have just a handful of years in which children accept that magic is possible, and to crush their dreams too early is a crime.

My sister Emma, four years older than me, once sought out our mother and demanded to know the truth about Christmas. She was seized by fear that she may, as an adult, not provide any presents for her children, then discover that none had appeared overnight. Even worse, apparently, was the concern that she might go to all the trouble of buying gifts, only to wake up on Christmas morning to a surfeit of stockings. Our mother sympathised with her dilemma and told Emma the truth, and I can only assume she kept it to herself, because I have no recollection of the point at which I discovered the truth about Father Christmas. Instead I drifted from childhood into teens with my eyes tightly shut each Christmas Eve, feeling the magic as my stocking was gently placed across my feet, even once I knew it was my parents who crept upstairs, quietly cursing the squeaky floorboards. The truth was known, but never spoken.

This is what I hoped for my children.

Not that they remained naïve enough to genuinely believe in Santa, but that they were able to retain the spirit of Christmas, and the magic of tradition, for as long as possible. So if your offspring are older, and have long-since abandoned frivolities such as stockings, tread carefully around those parents with wide-eyed children and magic in their hearts. Whisper the truth to your own kids if you wish, but implore them to keep it to themselves. Let other children believe in magic for just a little while longer.

Dressed to impress

A Christmas tree decorated by children is a wonderful thing, isn't it? Gold ribbon lovingly draped across the branches, family treasures rescued from tissue paper and strung on silver thread. A Sunday evening filled with laughter and happiness, with King's College choir on CD and the log fire crackling, as one's offspring joyfully carry on family traditions at this most magical time of year.

Except there's no fire, because you forgot to order a load from Logs R Us, and you're not giving an arm and a leg to Daylesford for kiln-dried, hand-turned logs you'll burn in a day. And the kids have rebelled against the beauty of King's College, and have insisted on the *Frozen* soundtrack.

Again.

Oh, and the tree's a disaster. Because let's face it: Christmas trees decorated by children look . . . well, shit.

If you made the mistake of letting the kids actually choose the tree, it's either ten foot tall and now bent over beneath the ceiling, or it's a stubby bush with not even a nod to symmetry or grace. Around this lurid green shrub will now be wrapped several yards of tinsel you thought you'd thrown out years ago. The baubles – those that haven't been broken – will be gathered so far to the left that the entire tree is now listing to one side, despite a whole day spent wedging tiny pieces of wood into the stand to keep it upright. It looks drunk. You're tempted to join it.

One side of the tree will be totally bare. There will be no lights at the top whatsoever, but so many clustered together at the bottom you can't look at them without thinking of Gestapo interrogation rooms. To add insult to injury, every decoration the children have ever made will have found a home on the branches.

'Where's the wise man's camel?' Josh asked me one year.

'What wise man's camel?' I said, playing for time.

'The one I made at pre-school.'

'Do you mean the egg box with the piece of yellow string stuck on one side?'

'Yes,' he said impatiently, 'the wise man's camel.'

'Um, I think I packed it away in my special box in the loft,' I said, knowing full well I put it in the recycling at least two years ago.

It was a satisfactory answer – it always is.

At some stage the children will catch on to the fact that, given my less than enthusiastic response to the armfuls of tat they bring home from school, it is highly unlikely I am packing it up and squirrelling it away in the loft for safe keeping. I don't have a special box. I don't even have a box. Evie once poked her head into the loft when I was looking for a suitcase.

'Where's the special box full of all our stuff?' she asked.

'It's that one,' I said swiftly, pointing to the largest and most impressive cardboard box, which – when I last looked – contained Rob's old cricketing whites, a broken television and a full set of Linguaphone Spanish cassette tapes.

'Wow,' she said, her eyes widening, 'and it's full of all our treasures?'

'It certainly is,' I said firmly, ushering her back down the ladder and shutting the loft hatch.

If I kept the wise man's camel, I'd have to keep it all. The fairy made out of yoghurt pots, the papier-mâché Father Christmas, and the myriad salt-clay discs with glitter-filled handprints. The tree would collapse under the strain, and that's assuming it survived the sheer embarrassment of looking like it's been vomited on by a Hobbycraft catalogue.

Of course the children love decorating the tree, and there's no reason why they can't. But come nine o'clock, when the *Frozen* CD has finished its fourth loop, and the kids have trooped off to bed, it's down to work. Off with the tinsel, the fairy lights and the lopsided baubles, and back on with artfully, intelligently placed objects of beauty.

Last year the children raced down at first light to turn on the lights and gaze at the tree they had so lovingly decorated the night before.

'It looks so beautiful,' Evie said in awe. Her siblings sighed with happiness.

'Although it looks sort of . . .' George hesitated. 'Sort of *different*.'

There was a pause, and I held my breath. Had I been

too obvious? Too bold? Josh's eyes scanned the tree from tip to trunk.

'It's not different,' he said with conviction, 'we just did an even better job than we thought we did.'

Home-made Christmas

What is it about Christmas that means everything has to be home-made, anyway? Sure, the hard-core crafters make birthday cards all year round, dye hard-boiled eggs for Easter breakfasts, and crochet heart-shaped bunting in preparation for Valentine's Day, but at Christmastime the stakes are really raised.

This week, in amongst the usual mince pie recipes and egg nog serving suggestions, I've seen instructions for home-made advent calendars, hand-stamped wrapping paper, papier-mâché tree decorations, and a step-by-step guide to knitting your own nativity scene.

Who comes up with it all? Is it Kirstie Allsopp?

Is it not enough that we have to find inspiration for eleventy billion presents, source sufficient tat to fill the children's stockings, remember to order the turkey and drive round the county hand-delivering cards because we've missed the last post? Apparently not. Now I'm made to feel inadequate if the wreath on my front door hasn't been lovingly crafted from locally sourced greenery and decorated with ribbons from my thrift box. Hell, I'm made to feel inadequate because I don't even *have* a thrift box.

I blame Pinterest. I'm a big fan of social media, as you'll know if you've ever witnessed the Olympic-standard levels of procrastination I achieve on Twitter when I'm supposed to be writing, but there's no doubt it's the scourge of the modern woman, and particularly of the modern woman with neither the time, the inclination nor the skill to create a shabby-chic Christmas tree stand from an upcycled wine crate. Type 'Christmas' into Pinterest and stand well back, before your screen erupts in an explosion of red, green, silver and gold creations I can only conclude have been uploaded with the sole intention of causing widespread depression.

'So cute!' exclaims the caption beneath a tree-topper angel, engineered from a retro Sindy doll and dressed in a ballgown made from scraps of baby clothes.

'I can't wait to do this with my little one's outfits!' someone has commented.

I want to message her and ask her if she's really going to make what is actually a fairly hideous-looking decoration, or whether she's secretly rolling her eyes like I am.

'You know you can just *buy* tree-topper dolls, don't you?' I want to post.

But of course I don't. Because that's the big secret of social media, isn't it? No one really lives the life they allow to play out online. We share links for blog posts explaining how to combine unwanted jumpers and your surplus harvest of lavender into festive hand-warmers, just as we post photos of our smiling children taken in a fleeting interlude between screaming matches. There's no more substance in the assertion that we've 'collected so many glass jars – time for Christmas pickling!' than there is in the bold end-of-term status update that claims we're 'looking forward to two whole weeks of family time!' (thumbs up, smiley face).

I'm putting an end to it.

I hereby solemnly declare and affirm that not one part of the Mackintosh Christmas this year will be home-made. I will have stacks of supermarket mince pies, and enough shop-bought sloe gin that no one will care. I'll buy whatever crackers go with the tablecloth, and any wrapping paper available on a three-for-two. Someone else can spend time soaking my fruit cake in liquor and smoothing out the wrinkles in the marzipan, and I couldn't give two hoots if it isn't served on a plate sporting my children's handprints cunningly transformed into a reindeer. The kids' advent calendars will be a collection of straightforward windows, not heirlooms with gifts behind each wooden door.

In short, Christmas will come in a series of supermarket bags, and I will refuse to be shamed by the plethora of crafting blogs, hobby magazines and Pinterest posts. If God had meant us to make our own brandy butter, He wouldn't have invented Waitrose.

Home truths

It's happened. I've been discovered. Perhaps I was foolish to think that my lies might be safe for another year at least – after all, it was inevitable that I'd be found out eventually – but nonetheless I am distraught. I had hoped for more time. For ten years I've justified the lying, the cheating, the sneaking around. I've crept upstairs at midnight, holding my breath as the stairs creak, desperately trying to keep my nocturnal wanderings a secret, bracing myself for a figure at the top of the stairs. *What are you doing? Where have you been?* Yet somehow I've got away with it. Until now.

It should never have happened. Not like this. I was careful – too careful to get caught. No, like so many women in my situation, I was unmasked by someone else. I feel a swell of anger when I think about it; about the self-righteousness of it all. What right do other people have to interfere in my business? In my relationships?

It was a child who shopped me, of all people. A teenager. Defending their actions as *doing the right thing, telling the truth, setting the record straight*, when in reality their motivations were far more mischievous. Stirring up trouble. Dropping me in it. Light the blue touch paper and stand well back. He knew full well what would happen, and he did it anyway.

'Father Christmas isn't real,' he announced.

I wasn't there, but I can picture the teenager's gleeful mug; the consequent confusion on my own son's face. Only four years between them, yet those years forming an almost tangible bridge between child and near-adult. 'It's your parents who get all the presents. Your parents who fill the stockings.'

Years of white lies – of stories, of make-believe – felled by loose-lipped words. I imagine my son's jaw quivering a little; the tiny muscles around his eyes tensing as he tried to make sense of what he was hearing. Did it come as a shock, or had he always suspected? Had someone tried to tell him once before? Only he believed in magic, back then, and he was happy to dream about tooth fairies and flying reindeer; quick to dismiss the suggestion that his parents could have had anything to do with the bulging stocking on his bed each Christmas morning. Why, we were as amazed as he was by its arrival! We marvelled over each tiny present, just as he did! And how else could each item from his list (written in secret and handed solemnly to his mother to post) appear on Christmas Day, if not by magic, if not at the hands of Father Christmas?

But he is older now. Tainted by real life, by the grown-up books he reads, the films he watches, the friends he sees at school and at home. He listens to the news on the radio each morning, and asks me why there are still bombs falling, wars raging. He knows the world is not perfect; he knows people break laws, bend truths, tell lies. Magic has left him, slowly but surely as each year has passed.

Father Christmas isn't real.

This time he listened. This time it was the teenager he believed, not the fairy tale. Not me.

'Is it true?' he asked me.

Tears stung my eyes. I wanted to lie. I wanted to cling on to his childhood because suddenly it felt as though it was about more than just Christmas fables; it was about growing up. Becoming an adult.

I thought. Took a deep breath. Chose each word with the care the occasion deserved. 'It would be difficult for anyone,' I said, 'however magic they are – to be in so many places at once.'

'But is it true?' he persisted. 'The stockings . . . all the presents . . . Is it you who buys them?' Silence, like thick snow.

I remember each and every stocking. I remember each gift I placed in them; each joyful smile as they were unwrapped. I remember peeling off price stickers and running out of Sellotape and forgetting the satsumas and . . . What now? What would I do now? I looked at his face, so open and trusting, and I knew that if I lied about this, he would never believe me again.

'It's true.'

He nodded. Deliberations flickered behind his eyes and I wanted to reach in and catch them; to know how he felt, what he thought about this revelation. And then, as though he had been shoved from behind, he threw himself at me, his arms tight around my neck and his cheek hot against mine.

'Thank you,' he said. 'Thank you for all the presents. You're amazing.'

Christmas past

My mother tells me that when I was little we would trek down to Devon to spend Christmas Day with my grandparents, but I have no recollection of those years. My childhood memories of Christmas are all held within the family home: in the corner of the sitting room where the tree stood; in the dining room with its table extended far into the hall; in the hearth where the men of the house would stand, warming their backs against the fire.

Christmas Eve has always been special: a quiet celebration of family time, with an enormous cold salmon and a table lit with candles. Traditions were added, but none ever removed, and the air would be filled with promise. We three children would receive our stockings from our mother; a leg each from pairs of American tan tights, guaranteed to stretch excitingly around the most obscurely shaped gift. We would skip about the house, twirling and whirling our stockings about us, until we were sent to bed to toss and turn, hearing the grandfather clock strike the hours and willing sleep to come before we heard the tread of the stairs.

I would wake before first light, eyes still closed as I tested for the gloriously heavy sensation across my legs which meant Father Christmas had been. I would climb out of bed, dragging my stocking behind me and revelling in the dull thump it made as it hit the floor. Out on the landing I might meet my sisters, and together we would make the decision to wake the parents. Was it too early? Would we be allowed in? One of us would creak open their bedroom door with a stage-whispered request that was almost always met with acceptance, if not unbridled enthusiasm, and together we would take up residence in their room to exclaim about each carefully retrieved present.

My mother would check on the turkey, returning with a wail that once again the oven hadn't turned itself on overnight and we would be eating late. In time, that four o'clock lunch was so enjoyed by us all it became a tradition in itself, long after the family oven was replaced with a more reliable one. Grandparents would show up around midday, patiently receiving each of us in turn for a display of our stocking presents. There would be more presents; children disappearing under a sea of discarded paper, more chaos, more laughter. There would be tears – always tears – through tiredness or disappointment, but short-lived in the main. But above all there would be love. Love that wrapped itself around every present chosen, every dish cooked, every Christmas kiss and comforting cuddle. My mother, drinking gin and tonic from a cut-crystal glass as she cooked up a storm in the kitchen. My father, holding court over lunch with anecdotes that had us all in stitches. A place at the table for anyone who wanted one.

And now I am grown, and I have three children of my

own, and Christmas traditions are changing. But I will cut the legs of American tan tights bought expressly for the purpose of Christmas stockings, and my children will whirl and twirl with them about the house until I chase them into bed with a threat that Father Christmas comes only to sleeping children. Their father and I will nibble Rudolph teeth-marks in the carrot, drink the milk and scatter mince-pie crumbs about the table, just as my own parents did all those years ago.

We will creep upstairs to lay three stockings at the ends of three little beds, and groan when morning comes too soon for such excited chatter. The memories we create for our children are descended from all those years of joy-filled Christmases at home, and if I do half as good a job as my own parents did, I know they will treasure them for ever.

NEW BEGINNINGS

For last year's words belong to last year's language
And next year's words await another voice . . .
And to make an end is to make a beginning.

T. S. Eliot

The pattern of our year is led largely by the seasons. By the way spring feeds into summer; the way summer, in turn, gives way to autumn and then winter. We are pulled from one event to another – from Valentine's Day to Mothering Sunday; from Summer Solstice to Hallowe'en – and we mark the months that pass with increasing wonder. *How can it be May already? Can you believe it's October next week? This year has simply flown by.*

Time hastens unfairly the less we have of it, and the long lazy summers of our childhoods fly by in a heartbeat.

It is important, then, at the end of the year, to reflect upon what we have done – what we have achieved in spite of such hurtling days. Children grow, move on, move out. Friendships are made, and occasionally broken; and happiness ebbs and flows, as it is wont to do. We have sown and reaped, this year; baked and eaten, loved and lost. We have treated each month as the gift it has been.

My family has grown up within the pages of this book, and amid the honeyed stone of our Cotswold town. Three children, grown from toddler to teen. Chickens, dogs, guinea pigs. Family days, birthdays, and oh-so-many Christmases. We have laughed and cried, argued and made up. We have changed as each season came in, as each year rolled by.

So many changes.

But the biggest of all is yet to come.

Moving on

It is moving day. The news comes with a maelstrom of emotions I hadn't expected. Excitement, of course: a new house, a new adventure. But a wave, too, of something more akin to bereavement than it should be; this is, after all, a house we are losing, not family. Not a child. Yet a loss it is, the kind that tugs at your heart with the life you're leaving behind, that sidles up to you and flicks through an album of memories.

Our old house was itself a new start, back when life was dark with the aftermath of our son's death, and the way forward was tentative and painful. A house to begin life as a family of three, not four; a house empty of associations. I packed every box myself, seven-month-old Josh by my side, kicking his legs in the air. I labelled and listed and watched our belongings being loaded into the van, before we drove half a mile up the road to our new house – to this house. Still in Chipping Norton, but bigger – so much bigger, with a garden, and room for trikes and footballs and whatever else was in our future. No more children; of that we were certain. No more IVF, no more doctors and poking and prodding about. Counting our blessings instead.

Little did we know I was already pregnant. As I lugged a mattress up the stairs, put the Ikea wardrobe together, leaned precariously over the banister to paint the stairwell. All the while, there was more life inside me. Two heartbeats, biding their time. Waiting to make their presence known.

And now here we were; a family of five, in this house we have loved but finally outgrown. A house that saw three children start school; become people in their own right. A house in which I became a writer.

Within its four walls we made plans that never came to fruition, and many that grew wings. There is so much I will miss about living here. We have grown too big, as a family, for these rooms, but there is nevertheless comfort in their familiarity. I can pad downstairs in the dead of night, surefooted in the darkness. Avoiding the creaky step, reaching for a glass to fill from the tap. I know every noise, every sigh and moan from the trees in the woods beside us. The bark of the foxes; the cows in the fields.

As we spent our final days in the house I found myself stopping work and listening, drinking in the sounds we would soon be leaving behind. Next door's car arriving home; the garage door opposite being opened, then shut. A child playing somewhere in the street.

It is a friendly place to live. I will miss the neighbours. They have taken in parcels without complaint, and thrown back the footballs that spend more time in their gardens than in ours. They were there when I locked myself out; when I was late back from work and there was no one to watch the kids. For nine years they have been a constant presence in our lives, and I will miss them terribly.

There is one final pocket of grief that pulls at my heart; one I am resolutely trying to ignore. I am turning away from the album of memories thrust in my face, the slide-show of photos taunting me, the voice needling me. *Won't you miss this?* it says.

I sneak a glance. Catch my breath. Rolling hills, in hues of green and gold. Golden stone houses offering slices of sunny warmth even on the greyest days. Market towns and farmers' markets. Snapshots of a landscape unrivalled.

How could you move away from this? the voice whispers.

Because this new chapter in our lives – this new house we have bought – is a hundred miles away.

We didn't plan to leave the Cotswolds. It just sort of happened. A casual browse through Rightmove, late one night when the walls were closing in on me and I craved space like an addict after her next fix.

Let's move house. Let's find another Cotswold house, with a garden, and space for the children, and somewhere the dog basket won't get knocked every time the back door's opened.

A local search. Let's say . . . a five-mile radius.

Oh. Nothing within budget. How can houses cost that much? What are they made of, gold? Are they built upon oil wells? Did Charles Dickens once live there? £1.2 million for *the perfect weekend retreat*? We don't want a weekend retreat. We want a home.

Clicking further afield: Herefordshire, Worcestershire . . .

Wales. *Wales*? Well, how ridiculous. We're hardly likely to move to Wales. It's miles from everyone we know, miles from family, miles from friends. It rains all the time, and I have it on good authority that they all speak Welsh. Why on earth would we look at a house in Wales?

Although the countryside is beautiful, and wouldn't it be nice to be nearer to the sea? A quick peek, then. Just to see what's out there.

Goodness, look at that floor plan . . . look at those photos . . . look at the *space*! Perhaps it wouldn't hurt to ask for a viewing; just for comparison's sake. Not to buy: just to look. Houses are never as nice as they seem from the photos, after all.

Oh gosh, it really *is* that spectacular . . .

So that was how it happened. Like the Swallows and Amazons who didn't mean to go to sea, we didn't mean to move to Wales. But there's a skip in my step when I think of the mountains of Snowdonia, and a glow in my heart when I see the light glistening on the lake. A bedroom each for the children, a playroom, a boot room. A writing room free from bills and admin and other people's mismatched socks, a room with space for all my books. A new town to explore, and memories to be made. A new language to learn.

It'll be all right, won't it? Those of you who have relocated, who have moved a hundred miles or more away, it'll be okay, right? We'll make new friends, yet keep the old ones. We'll find new haunts, but come back often to our Cotswold favourites. Won't we?

Tell me it will all be fine, because I want so badly for

this to work. I didn't mean to leave the Cotswolds, but Snowdonia is waiting with open arms, and I think – I hope – we're going to be as happy there as we have been here.

POSTSCRIPT

The real voyage of discovery consists, not in seeking new lands, but seeing with new eyes.

Marcel Proust

Two years have passed since a moment of spontaneity took us away from the Cotswolds and into the mountains of Snowdonia. When I broke the news to friends and family that we were moving, the response was consistent and predictable.

'You do know it rains in Wales?'

'It rains everywhere,' I replied gaily.

Chipping Norton was hardly the Costa del Cotswolds, after all. Muddy walks and wet school runs were part and parcel of our winters (and frequently our summers) in Oxfordshire, and so they would continue to be in North Wales. I doubted I'd even notice the change in climate.

Oh my God: THE RAIN!

It pours down for hours, days, weeks at a time. It gushes down drainpipes, rushes along pavements, and puddles into every available pothole. Two months after our move, I couldn't remember the last time I'd returned from a dog walk without wet trousers, wet socks, wet *underwear*, for heaven's sake.

Was it climate change? The apocalypse? Or was it just . . . North Wales?

I heard the warnings of my naysayer friends echoing in my ears. Why hadn't I listened?

And then something struck me. As I set out on yet another wet dog walk, water seeping between my damp collar and my neck, it occurred to me that, in the midst of these biblical rains, I hadn't heard anyone else complaining about them. Not a soul.

'Not a bad day today, is it?' the lady in the newsagent said one morning. I followed her gaze out of the window, over which water was cascading from the gutter above. On the high street, a woman was battling with an umbrella, drenched from the waist down by passing cars driving through the puddles.

'Not as wet as yesterday,' the newsagent continued.

And I had to give her that; it was indeed marginally less wet than the previous day, when I had contemplated borrowing a kayak and paddle to splash my way down the street from our house to the shops. *Not as wet as yesterday*.

As the week progressed, and the rain continued to pour, I realised the newsagent was not the only Pollyanna in the village.

'Lovely and mild today!' declared a man with an enthusiastic retriever.

And indeed it was. Positively balmy, if one compared

it to – say – Iceland. It seems that, in North Wales, weather is just a state of mind.

Relocation was not without its problems. As one friend – subjected to our many tales of gazumping, mortgage refusals and survey horrors – put it, 'This has been the most stressful house move I never made.' But eventually it was happening, and the anxiety of whether the purchase would go through gave way to fevered interior-design dreams in which Laurence Llewelyn-Bowen arrived with books of wallpaper samples and insisted the dog pick out her favourites. We let ourselves loose in online stores and laughed at John Lewis sofas with names reminiscent of Cotswold children. Archie, Tilly, Oslo. Conran Marlowe Large.

And then, finally, came moving day, and the excitement of the liveried House & Carriage lorries trundling up the drive of the new house. I put the kettle on the Aga and listened to the screams of excitement from our children as they played hide-and-seek across three floors of a house that already felt like home.

There were ups and downs along the way; new friends made, and tears shed for old ones.

'We'll see them again,' I promised when the children were homesick, and I thought of the friends I missed myself.

When summer came, our thoughts turned to holidays. 'Where would you like to go?' I asked the children. They exchanged hopeful glances, eyes lighting up with excitement.

'The Cotswolds!' they said as one.

★

We take our home towns for granted, don't we? Long-time Londoners confess they rarely take in a show, or visit the myriad museums on their doorstep. Stratfordians admit they've never quite got round to seeing Anne Hathaway's cottage.

I lived within striking distance of both Oxford and London for almost forty years, yet the only time I've been on an open-top bus tour (which remains one of the most brilliant ways to see a city) was the summer I spent working as an English teacher for a language college. I loved that summer. Not only did I get to use a guillotine *and* a laminator (by far the best motivation for joining the profession, as far as I can see), but I got to take young people out sight-seeing. I went punting in Oxford and Cambridge; visited the National Portrait Gallery, the Ashmolean, Blenheim Palace, Buckingham Palace and Hampton Court; wandered around Stratford, Cheltenham, Windsor and Bath; and learned how to swear in seventeen different languages. It was an exhausting, exhilarating, educational summer, in which I saw more of my home county and the surrounding area than I had seen in my entire life to date.

When I joined the police and was posted to Oxford, I revelled in my time patrolling the ancient streets. Like many of my colleagues, I felt honoured to wander college grounds, and was patiently indulgent of American tourists asking for directions to 'Oxford University'. *I must go to the Ashmolean again some time,* I would think as I drove up St Giles' on my way to a job.

I never did.

Familiarity breeds contempt, and when something's on your doorstep it's all too easy to walk past it. Tomorrow. Next week. Some other time. When I lived in Chipping Norton there was a lot I saw and did, but there was a lot I didn't. I didn't make the most of having a theatre around the corner; I didn't make the most of the high-street shops. I didn't once go to Westonbirt Arboretum, even though every autumn I said we must. I didn't visit Chastleton House, just a few miles from home, or take the kids to the falconry centre.

Now that the Cotswolds is a holiday destination, and not our home, we scour the horizon for honey-stone cottages, bouncing in our seats at familiar road signs. *Oxfordshire! Shipston-on-Stour! Great Rollright!* We take the scenic route from friend to friend, so the children can spy on their old school, and I can watch the rolling hills from the car window and think of all the dog walks I meant to try and somehow never did. We visit every tea shop in Chipping Norton, rallying nostalgia back and forth across the table. *Remember when Josh choked on his hot chocolate? When Evie was sick in your hat? When you said you didn't want cake and then you had it anyway?* The most mundane of memories made special because of where they are shared. So many things we did and saw, yet so much more we could have done.

Wherever you live, take time to see your home town through the eyes of a visitor. Look through the rack of leaflets at the train station and find an attraction you haven't even heard of. Put your phone in your pocket and look up at the buildings around you, find something in your high street you've never seen before, buy from a shop you've never once set foot in.

With friends to see, and family to visit, my own time 'back home' goes far too fast. Before long we're back in the car again, watching the buttery stone fade away, and the road stretch out before us.

I always feel lost for a while, as though I've been ripped from one world and not yet placed in another. Then, gradually, the grey stone, slate-topped buildings of North Wales begin to appear, and the hills become mountains. A new chapter. A new life. A new home.

Acknowledgements

My sincere thanks to Rhiannon Smith at Little, Brown, for her creative and enthusiastic approach to this project, and to Zoe Gullen and Sarah Shrubb for helping to make it happen. Thanks, too, to my agent Sheila Crowley, and to the Curtis Brown team who work so hard on my behalf.

I have loved being a columnist for *Cotswold Life*, and remain so grateful to the editors, Mike Lowe and Candia McCormack, for giving an unknown writer such a fantastic opportunity. Thank you.

Finally, the biggest of thank yous to my friends, neighbours and colleagues in the Cotswolds, who provided so much inspiration for my columns, and made Chipping Norton the most wonderful place to live and work. I miss you all very much.

I have donated my advance for this book to the Silver Star Society, a charity based at the John Radcliffe Hospital, without which I would not have a family at all.

Clare Mackintosh

Epigraphs

January: Sara Coleridge, 'The Months'
February: William Morris, *The Earthly Paradise*
March: Lewis Grizzard, *Getting' it On: A Down-Home Treasury* (Galahad Books, 1989)
April: proverb
May: William Shakespeare, *Henry IV, part one*
June: L. M. Montgomery, *Anne of the Island*
July: Francis Thompson, 'A Corymbus for Autumn'
August: Sylvia Plath, *The Journals of Sylvia Plath 1950–1962*, ed. Karen V. Kukil (Faber, 2000)
September: Alexander Theroux, *Darconville's Cat* (Henry Holt, 1996)
October: John Ruskin, 'The Months'
November: Cynthia Rylant, *In November* (Harcourt, 2000)
December: Christmas carol
New beginnings: T. S. Eliot, *Little Gidding* (Faber, 1942)
Postscript: Marcel Proust